25 Facts of God

Attributes and Applications

by
Matt Given

Monument, CO
80132

25 Facts of God
Attributes and Applications
Copyright © 2011 by Matt Given
All Rights Reserved

All italics within Scripture quotations have been added by the author. The author has also chosen to capitalize all the personal pronouns of God even if the original authors, quoted texts, and Biblical translations choose not to. This is merely a matter of personal preference that seemed appropriate for a book that aims to convey a higher and more respected view of God.

ISBN: 978-1-61314-030-7

Cover Design: PhilHerrold.com
Printed in the United States of America
First Edition: November 2011

Interested in hosting a one day or week-end seminar on the "25 Facts of God" for your church or weekend retreat?

Contact Matt for further information on hosting a "Week-End Walk Thru the Attributes of God"
25anchors@gmail.com or 25FactsofGod.com

"Bulk Rate" Sales Discounts
available at 25FactsofGod.com

25 Facts of God
Attributes and Applications

Our Biggest Problem

I have no idea what the biggest problem is in the universe. There may be a black hole in some far-off galaxy sucking everything into its endless void. There may be a renegade asteroid somewhere that is wreaking havoc in solar systems yet unseen and unknown to us. Light-years away, there may even be a battle raging between an evil galactic empire and a small band of rebels led by a three-foot-high green creature named Yoda. But I do know what the biggest problem is on *this* planet.

If you were to ask your friends, family, and co-workers what they believe is the world's biggest problem, you would get all kinds of answers. Poverty, injustice, greed, crime, abortion, war, climate change, natural disasters, and the other calamities of life would be some of the more popular answers. But none of these issues compare to our biggest problem – *the misconceptions people have about God.*

Why the Problem is a Problem
Of all the world's problems, how can this one possibly be the worst? It's because our thoughts about God affect everything about us. Our beliefs about God affect how we interpret every event in our lives and every news story on the world stage. Everything, absolutely everything that happens is interpreted and reacted to in one way or another.

Sometimes we react with action, but most often our response is seen only in our thoughts, our feelings, and the conclusions we then reach about the world around us. Our underlying view of God drastically impacts and influences our interpretation of every event in life.

We are mostly unaware of it, but our basic assumptions on hundreds of issues are largely based on our view of God. Our concept of God is a foundation upon which our moral choices are built. This is true for us as individuals and as a culture. Where our concept of God declines, so do our moral standards.[1] It is no exaggeration to say that our misconceptions about God force us to draw wrong conclusions on how we view life and the basic issues we face daily.

Faulty beliefs keep people from coming to God in faith. Tony Campolo loved to ask university students who were antagonistic about the Christian faith to describe the God who they did not believe existed. They were often confused by the very question. But eventually they would describe their version of "God." Their descriptions of Him were primarily tainted and one-sided, focusing almost exclusively on only one or two aspects of His character, most often His wrath or anger.

When they were finished, Tony would invariably look them in the eye and say something like, "I don't believe in that God either." He could do this because the God they would describe had very little in common with the God of the Bible. There is a frightening ignorance about God in our world today. Our thoughts and our understanding of Him are often faulty, mistaken, or just far too small.

3 Reasons for Our Wrong Thoughts about God
1. We allow our experiences and observations of the world to shape our opinions about Him. The disappointments and the tragic events of our past and the heartbreaking tragedies and catastrophes we see on the news every day lead millions to the conclusion that God does not exist.

And EVEN IF it is true that God does exist, many conclude that He is *not* a God who is in charge of or sovereign over the events of this world. He is certainly not a God who has a personal interest in each of us. The very last thing He is in the minds of many, is a God who has a passionate love for each of us.

2. We decide and create the God we want to believe in, one we're most comfortable with. If you don't like the idea of hell, your God is going to be exclusively merciful, gracious, and loving. This version of God only punishes those who murder, rape, or commit other "really bad" sins while the rest of us either skate into or slip into heaven depending on how good we were in this lifetime.

The opposite is true as well. For those actively embracing a lifestyle far from the desires of a holy God, their version of God is the cosmic killjoy who exists only to make sure they have less fun. Their lives are marked by open rebellion, where God is not loving, not forgiving, and not merciful. He is a God who is only waiting to swoop down upon them to unleash His fury. For either mindset, there is a direct connection between your view of God and your lifestyle.

3. We don't do well with the mystical and the things that cannot be fully known. We want to see and understand God in purely relational ways. We don't do well with the mystery of God, so He is seen and understood in ways we want to see and understand Him. We don't want our God to be an unknown quantity; we want Him to be more of a warm, loving, and kindly old grandfather.

We are often far too quick to shy away from the mystical aspects of God. We think that the only religions with a "mystical" element to them are the ones of the Far East. Many see Christianity as the well-reasoned, factually accurate, and totally figured-out faith. While true and defendable, Christianity must also have a mysterious element to it.

Our increasing knowledge of all we see (and even the things we cannot see due to their size or distance) lead us to the belief that *everything* can be known. There is no mystery any longer. With our scientific mindset, if we cannot measure it, test it, or observe it with our senses, then it does not exist. To us, seeing is believing. But a religion without mystery is a religion without God.

3 Reasons for Small Thoughts about God

1. We have shrunk God down to something we *can* conceive. In our effort to understand the majesty and incomprehensibility of God, we have shrunk Him down to something we *can* understand and wrap our brains around. But the truth is, no matter how smart we are, we will always be finite creatures with limited ability to understand the supernatural.

God is supernatural. He is majestic, infinite, and incomprehensible. You will never fully understand or comprehend the God of the Bible. Any version of God out there that is understandable and fully known is not the Almighty God of this reality.

This knowable version of God that we have created in our effort to better understand Him is not the God revealed to us in the Bible. This is also not the God of past generations. Today we have settled for a God with whom we are comfortable – one we have created because He is then manageable and knowable. But the problem with this kind of God is simple: He can never surprise us or leave us in speechless awe. He can never astonish or transcend us. He's far too small.[2]

2. We want a God of comfort. We are, to a large extent, a need-centered people. We want a Bible Study or a Sunday sermon that is going to fix our problems and make our lives easier. We want to feel better after leaving church each week. We may have drifted from teaching about *who God is*, to *what He can do for us*. If we're not careful we can become merely consumers of God, only using Him to meet our needs and grant us our desires.

6

The reality is, a God that only soothes our souls and gives us the security for which we all long is not the God who can also move mountains, heal the sick, bring revival, break the spirits of the proud, and cause the worst of sinners to fall to their knees. There is more to God than we have made Him out to be.

Our natural inclination is to desire a God who is a source of security. We are genetically prone to want a God of comfort. But we also want a God who is manageable. We want to be able to use Him for our own purposes. We want Him only when we need Him. We want a God we can have some control over. We like the feeling of security that comes from knowing what God is like. It makes us feel better to think we have God all figured out.[3]

3. We think we already know enough about God. Once the basics are covered, we're satisfied and content. We often live our lives with a knowledge of God that is limited by how much we need Him. When our lives are going well, we have little need of Him.

Once the gospel message is understood and accepted, once our salvation is assured and our "fire insurance" has been secured, our desire to learn more about the God who saves is far too easily quenched and far too often satisfied.

Reflection Questions:
1. What has shaped your beliefs about God – the Bible or your own history and observations?
2. Which wrong thought about God can you relate to most? Why?
3. Which small thought about God can you relate to most? Why?
4. How do you see others' opinions about God affecting their decisions?
5. How do your beliefs about God affect the conclusions you make about your life? The world?
6. How can your view of God shrink down your biggest problem?
7. Are you content with your current knowledge of God? Why?

"Think-On-It" Verse:
"The fool says in his heart, 'There is no God.'"
Psalm 14:1

Solutions, Challenges
& Rewards

The Solution: Change Your Way of Thinking

*"What comes into our minds when we think about
God is the most important thing about us."[1]*

This is how A.W. Tozer began one of the best books ever written on
the attributes of God. What he was saying was both simple and quite
profound. What you think about God defines you as a person.

What you think about God enables you to interpret the events of your
life and this world through a godly perspective. Right thoughts about
God will lead to right conclusions about His working in this world.
Wrong thoughts about God will lead to destructive conclusions about
the world in which we live. Our understanding of God's character is
not instinctual to us; it takes some effort on our part and transformed
thinking to truly know who God is.

The Biblical writers knew the importance of our thinking. Throughout
the Scriptures, we are encouraged to think rightly about God.

"Whatever is true, whatever is noble, whatever is right, whatever
is pure, whatever is lovely, whatever is admirable, if anything
is excellent or praiseworthy – *think about such things.*"
(Philippians 4:8)

Our natural inclination is to think upon the things of this world. Our
material comforts and natural pleasures usually find their way to the
top of the list. In fact, our natural way of thinking about our issues,
our natural way of thinking about God, *is* the problem. We must think
of God in bigger and even unnatural ways if we want truly
transformed lives.

"Do not conform any longer to the pattern of this world,
but be transformed by the *renewing of your mind.*"
(Romans 12:2)

We all recognize the need for transformed hearts. The problem is, we
want to take a shortcut. The Bible makes it clear: a transformed heart
comes through transformed thinking. We want to skip the
transformed thinking part and go straight to a transformed heart that
is fully healed, joyful, and at peace.

"Those who live according to the flesh have their minds set on what the flesh desires; but those who live in accordance with the Spirit have their minds set on what the Spirit desires. The mind governed by the flesh is death, but *the mind governed by the Spirit is life and peace.*"
(Romans 8:5-6)

The mind governed by God is a mind at peace. Our thinking about Him must be challenged if we are to be a people who live with joy and in peace despite our circumstances.

The Challenge: 5 Things You Need to Do

1. Let go of your desire to fully understand a God worthy of awe, silent reverence, and trust. When we know only a God who has no mystery about Him, we know a God who is not worth knowing. When we have a God who is all figured out, we have a God without majesty and magnificence. This is a God we will have a much harder time entrusting our lives with. A God without mystery is a God who is not big enough for us to place our faith in.

When I was a kid, my dad earned his pilot's license, and he decided to celebrate with a family plane ride. I was terrified; I mean, I was scared spitless. I had no fun, and I took no pleasure in looking out the plane window to see our tiny little house, my tiny little school, and the now miniaturized town in which we lived. Why?

Because I remembered what had happened a week earlier when our "pilot" had tried to panel our basement. It was not a scene that instilled a lot of confidence in me as a passenger. If this pilot had such a hard time cutting a straight line with a power saw, how could he ever land this plane?

You see, my dad had no mystery about him. I *could* comprehend him. My dad was a concept that I *could* wrap my brain around. He had no majesty; he had no "otherness" about him. That's why I was so scared. I was too familiar with him. In the same way, a God without mystery, a God we *can* comprehend, is a God who has been shrunk down in order for us to understand. It's impossible to fully trust our trials and our lives to that kind of God.

It is a good, and even necessary thing, that God has a sense of otherness and mystery about Him. When we avoid the mystery of God, we avoid the only God worthy of worship, honor, and praise. As Brennan Manning says, the challenge is for us to…

9

"reject the dignified, businesslike Rotary Club deity we chatter about on Sunday morning and search for a God worthy of awe, silent reverence, total commitment, and wholehearted trust."[2]

2. Recognize that using your emotions to decide what God is like is a foolish way to make a decision as big as this one. Deciding what God is like based on your own experience means making a decision based largely on emotion. In fact, deciding what God is like based on the tragic events of the world is also largely a very emotional decision, and emotions most of the time, can be misleading. Bringing God into the court of your reason is a foolish thing to do, especially when your reason and rationality are fueled by your emotion.

The next time you're at McDonald's, take a minute and look at the world around you through the straw you are about to drink from. You will see a very limited and narrow picture of everything that is around you. Focusing on the pain of your past or the tragedies of this world is like looking through a straw. There is much more than just the pain and disappointment that you may see. There is beauty, majesty, and evidences of a good and loving God everywhere.

Also realize the world in which you walk is not the world as God created it; sin has seriously disfigured it. We often blame God for the results of the poor decisions of others, but God has given us all the gift of freedom – and with that freedom comes the ability to suffer for others' foolishness. Don't respond emotionally to the results of people's stupidity. Don't base your opinions about God on the actions of sinful people living in a fallen world.

3. You need to be more aware of how *what* you think about God impacts others around you. Our concepts and beliefs about God leave a definite impression on those around us, and vice versa.

What are you known for? When others hear your name, what are the first thoughts that come to their minds? What's your reputation? Reflecting on the quote from Tozer – "what comes into our minds when we think about God is the most important thing about us" should challenge you to consider what comes to *others'* minds when they think about you and your thoughts about God.

We are a self-conscious people, but that's not always a bad thing; it forces us to become more aware of the impressions we leave on others. What impression about your God do you communicate to those you work with and those who live next door? How big is the God your unsaved family members see in you?

I remember what a sobering moment it was when I realized that my kids were old enough to remember events that I would rather they not. A big dentist bill came due, and my kids witnessed their dad walking around the house grousing about how much it would cost to fill their cavities. I did not handle it well. I didn't rant and rave or slam doors, but I was anxious, and they knew it.

That was not the impression I wanted to leave on my kids. What does my fear and frustration about our finances say to them about my God? It is a worn-out phrase, but "you are the only Bible many people will ever read." What do people read about your God as they watch you walk through this life?

But the opposite is also true. We tend to believe what others around us believe. We want to fit in, so the opinions of those around us tend to shape our own opinions as well. This is true for everyone, believers and non-believers alike.

You may have wonderful friends and attend a vibrant church that's buzzing with God-honoring activities, but there's still a good chance that those around you carry with them a tainted view of God. If their God is too small and all figured out, yours most likely will be also.

Don't dump your friends. Don't change churches. Don't do anything drastic. But do be more aware of how those around you think and how they conceive God to be. If you know some "big God" people, pursue them; then try to show your "small God" friends what a "big God" friend looks like.

But beware. The bigger your God, the bigger your prayers will become, and the bigger your hopes and visions for His kingdom will be. When this happens, those around you might grow a bit uncomfortable and cautious. It can be unsettling to others when you subtly challenge their assumptions and foundational understandings of what God is like.

4. Stop thinking human-fueled thoughts about God; they're far too small. The God of your brain, the God of your understanding, is but a shadow of the reality of God. Brennan Manning wrote:
> "The more we let go of our concepts and images of God, the bigger God grows and the more we approach the mystery of His

11

indefinability. When we overlook the dissimilarity, we begin to speak with obnoxious familiarity of the Holy, make ludicrous comments such as 'I can never imagine God doing such a thing,' calmly predict Armageddon, glibly proclaim infallible discernment of the will of God, and trivialize God, trimming the claws of the Lion of Judah."[3]

What Manning was implying is that we don't have God all figured out. I would humbly add to this thought: it's kind of arrogant to think that you have a firm grasp on who God is and how He works in this world.

This journey to understanding what God is like will continue throughout your lifetime. You will never stop learning. You will never stop growing. Your understanding will never plateau. Your knowledge and comprehension will continue to increase throughout your life. You will move forward, but you'll never get there. Your understanding will grow until this life is over and you find yourself in the very presence of the God about whom you've spent a lifetime learning. Then, and only then, will you finally realize how little you really knew about Him.

5. Do not assume your experiences with emotion carry over to God as well. We all experience emotion, God does also. But never assume that your experience with emotion is the same as His. We are finite, limited, temporal creatures who most often experience only one dominant emotion at a time.

Often in the course of describing God's attributes, we will hit on the topic of God and His emotions. God is not only infinite and eternal; He is transcendent. He experiences emotion in ways that are a deep and profound mystery to us. The encouragement here is not to place our experiences onto Him. It's short-sighted, and maybe even foolish, to assume that God's experiences with emotion are the same as ours.

The Reward: Our Lives are Made Easier

Wrong beliefs about God keep many non-believers from coming to Him. So if you're reading this as a skeptic, the Spirit of this God you don't believe in can show you who He truly is. But it's also vitally important for Christians to have an accurate understanding of God in order to see Him as He **really** is. The benefits of this proper understanding are huge. Tozer also wrote:

> *"The man who comes to a right belief about God is relieved of ten thousand temporal problems."*[4]

Who doesn't love the idea of being relieved of ten thousand temporal problems? But is it really true, or just an exaggeration to make a point? How does a better understanding of God change our situation and make life easier?

A right belief about God makes it easier to handle life's trials. A right belief about God makes Him much bigger than He was before. The God you can conceive and understand is limited in His power and abilities; the God of the Bible is not. The size of your God is inversely related to the size of your problems. A little God leads to big problems; a big God leads to little problems.

A right belief about God enables you to better recognize His sovereignty and plans for your life. You will have a divine perspective on your life and its trials. While your circumstances may not change, how you view them certainly will. You'll recognize that they do indeed have a purpose and that someone is in charge of the universe.

> "'For I know the plans I have for you,' declares
> the Lord, 'plans to prosper you and not to harm
> you, plans to give you hope and a future.'"
> Jeremiah 29:11

You don't face your trials by random chance. You'll discover there is a refining purpose and plan to the days that are ordained for you to live.

A right belief about God continually puts your focus on Him and not your circumstances. In the gospel account of Peter walking on water, everything was going great when his eyes were fixed on the Lord, but when he was distracted and decided to look at the waves crashing around him, (his circumstances) - he then began to sink.

Our eyes are usually on our circumstances and the waves crashing around us, not on God and His truth. This practice needs to stop if we really want a changed heart and a changed perspective.

Regardless of where you are in your journey, my hope is that this book will give you a bigger and more complete picture of who God is and what He does. No one is immune. No one has learned it all. Each of us needs to be challenged in the way we think about God.

Reflection Questions:

1. What are the first ten words you can think of to describe God?
2. What do these words you have chosen reveal about how you view God's character?
3. Why is what we think about God so important?
4. What do you want your God to look like? How might you have distorted Him in order to fill your desires?
5. Why is it so hard to let go of your desire to fully understand God and embrace His mysterious and mystical aspects?
6. Which of the five challenges is the most difficult for you?
7. How can a better understanding of the true character of God help you deal with your problems?

"Think-On-It" Verse:

"Do not conform any longer to the pattern of this world,
but be transformed by the renewing of your mind."
(Romans 12:2)

> "But will God really dwell on earth? The heavens,
> even the highest heaven, cannot contain You.
> How much less this temple I have built!"
> 1 Kings 8:27

1 - God is Infinite

Comprehending Infinity with Your "12 Sticks of Butter Brain"
On average, the human brain weighs about three pounds. It's an amazing part of your creation. It does incredible things for you all day long. It truly is a supercomputer unrivaled by anything we can build with our most advanced technology. But the bottom line is this: your brain weighs about the same as twelve sticks of butter. There is a definite downside to this arrangement.

You will never comprehend infinity with a brain like that. And since God is an infinite Being, you will never fully understand this aspect of Him with your finite brain, even if you use every ounce of your three pounds.

The infinite nature of God means that He exists outside of, and is not limited by, time or space. He is *without limits*. When we refer to God's infinite nature, we're usually talking about His "omni" qualities – His omniscience, His omnipotence, and His omnipresence. (He knows everything, He can do anything, and He is everywhere.) But remember that His infinity is not limited to these three characteristics.

But when we say God is everywhere and infinite, we also need to be specific. It would be pantheistic to say God **is** everything. God is not found in the trees, in a giraffe, or in a rock. His power is displayed through the creation of the trees, giraffes, and even rocks, but those things are not to be worshipped; only God is to be worshipped because He created all these things in His infinite power.

The "Sloppy Talk" Problem
At times we fall into sloppy talk in our conversations; we inadvertently use the wrong words at the wrong time. When kids use the wrong words we may find it kind of cute. My son used to refer to contacts as "eye-tacts" and my daughter used to speak of herself in the third person, but they grew out of it and now they talk much more gooder.

For example, you may be hesitant to speak another language you are learning because you don't want to mess up and sound foolish with your own sloppy talk. It can also be seen in our exaggerations. When we say, "I'm so hungry I can eat a horse," we are purposely exaggerating; we are aware of what we are doing. But sloppy talk also happens when we exaggerate without being aware of it.

Against great odds, the U.S. Olympic Hockey team won the gold medal in 1980. Since then it's been commonly referred to as "The Miracle on Ice." Really? A miracle? If that truly was a miracle, then the word is in serious danger of losing its true meaning.

We can do the same thing with the word *infinite*. It can lose its true meaning. We say, "She has infinite patience with her kindergarten class" or even, "There are an infinite number of stars." We often use the word infinite to mean "a lot" or even "countless." So what's the problem? The problem is that technically, the word *infinite* cannot be used of any created thing.

Everything that exists had a beginning; except God. Everything that you see will have an end; except God. When the word *infinite* is used as a quantitative adjective for something that can be measured, it's misused, and this misuse can then lead to a distortion of this attribute of God. Everything else can be measured except God.[1]

The Big Question: Can the Infinite God be Known?
If infinity can never really be comprehended, can the infinite God be known to His finite people? Writer R.C. Sproul explains how we deal with what is called the incomprehensibility of God.

> "It may suggest to us that since the finite cannot 'grasp' the infinite, that we can know nothing about God. If God is beyond comprehension, does that not suggest that all our religious talk is only so much theological babbling and that we are left with, at best, an altar to an unknown God? ... Rather it means that our knowledge is partial and limited, falling short of a total or comprehensive knowledge. The knowledge that God gives of Himself through revelation is both real and useful. We can know God to the degree that He chooses to reveal Himself."[2]

God can be known. He has chosen to reveal Himself to us through the special revelation of His word and through the observance of His creation. The infinite God reveals Himself to His finite creatures every moment of every day.

This infinite God has also revealed Himself to us through the person and work of Jesus Christ. In a very tangible way, the infinite walked

16

among the finite. This more than anything else, makes knowing the infinite God a reality.

Infinite and Intimate at the Same Time

God is infinite, so He will always be beyond our full comprehension, but it's also necessary to point out another amazing aspect of God: He is both infinite *and* intimate. He is a very personal God. While He is infinite and not subject to any of the limitations of humanity or creation, He is still personal. He interacts with us as individuals and we can relate to Him in an intimate way. "We can pray to Him, worship Him, obey Him, and love Him, and He can speak to us, rejoice in us, and love us."[3]

This is important for two reasons: First, it shows that our God is not just some unconcerned cosmic observer who started the planet spinning and then walked away to let it fend for itself. God is intimately involved in sustaining His creation (Hebrews 1:3).

Secondly, the fact that God is both imminent and transcendent sets the Christian religion apart from every other belief system. Our Almighty Infinite God is also our Abba Caring Father. No other world religion dares make this claim about its god.[4]

The Need for Balance

It is vitally important for us to remember that God covers the entire spectrum of infinite to intimate. Because of this, we also need to give balanced attention to both aspects. We tend to gravitate to one extreme or the other. God is not your buddy. He is much more.

Because He is infinitely powerful, we should be filled with a deep sense of awe. Because He is infinitely loving, we should be filled with a recognition that He cares for us and our needs. Focusing on one aspect too heavily gets us out of balance and distorts our view of the character of God.

Why "God is Infinite" is a BIG DEAL

Why is the infinite nature of God such a big deal? It's presented here as the first attribute for a reason. What makes this attribute so amazing is that by its very definition, it impacts all of the others. The third Tozer quote worth remembering explains this quite well.

*"Because God's nature is infinite, everything
that flows out of it is infinite also."* [5]

If God is infinite, then everything else about Him must also be infinite. He has no boundaries. He is without measure. He is without end. This is true of every one of His attributes.

As you read through the following attributes, continually remind yourself that God is all of these things to an infinite degree. He is not partially anything. Everything God is, He is in the extreme. To drive this point home further, here are all these truths listed in one place.

His holiness is boundless.	His love will never run out.
His mercy is without end.	His grace will never be exhausted.
His justice never quits.	He is not like us and never will be.
He can do anything.	He knows everything.
He is everywhere.	He never changes.
He is always in control.	He is never dependent on anyone.
His wisdom is never wrong.	He never needs anything or anyone.
His faithfulness will never end.	His goodness is unlimited.
His forgiveness is unceasing.	He has no beginning or end.
His jealousy is never satisfied.	His humility is measureless.
He is forever patient.	He desires relationship with you.
He is the only truthful.	He is eternally happy.

Reflection Questions:

1. How have you limited God? How have you shrunk Him down in order to better understand Him?
2. In light of God's infinite nature, what does Romans 5:20 mean?
3. What characteristic of God are you most thankful is found in an infinite supply?
4. How does this thankfulness play out in your life?
5. Where is your view of God on the "fear to familiar" scale? Is He cold and distant (too feared) or is He known and taken for granted (too familiar)?

    (Feared) 1   2   3   4   5   6   7   8   9 (Familiar)
6. Why might it be a bit disconcerting for some to read, "God is not your buddy?"
7. Because God is infinite, I will . . .

"Think-On-It" Verse:

"'Can anyone hide in secret places so that I cannot see him?' declares the Lord. 'Do not I fill heaven and earth?' declares the Lord."
Jeremiah 23:24

"But just as He who called you is holy, so be holy in all you do; for it is written: 'Be holy, because I am holy.'"
1 Peter 1:16

2 - God is Holy

What Separates Us from God?

God is not like us. Don't skip over that sentence with a "no duh" kind of response. Read it slowly and let it fully sink in. God is not like us. This is because He is holy, and we are not.

God's holiness is what separates us from Him. God is holy, and we are not. We think, and have always been taught, that our sin is what separates us from God, and this is true. Our inherited-from-birth, sinful state is the problem. Our sin is what keeps us from walking with Him in the garden as Adam and Eve once did.

But when we say that our sin separates us from God, the emphasis is put on *our* deficiency and *our* sin problem. The attention is placed on how *our* defilement has left us separated from the Holy One. The focus then becomes what *we* can do to fix the problem, what *we* can do to be reconciled with God. We have a debt that must be paid if we want to make things right with God. This is all true. But this perspective tends to put the focus on *our sin,* NOT on the holiness of God.

But when we start this conversation by saying "His holiness is what separates us from God," the spotlight is rightly put back on God and not our sin. God is holy, and that holiness cannot be compromised by the presence of our sin. Our attention is then placed back where it truly belongs; on the holiness of God. The focus then rightly becomes, what can a holy God do to have fellowship with a fallen people?

Some would say we're just playing with words: "It's six of one and half-dozen of another." But it's a matter of where your focus and your attention are drawn. Too often the focus skews toward our sin and not on the holiness of God. Think about it differently; think about it in this "backwards" way if you will. It's not our sin that separates us from God; it's God's holiness that separates Him from us.

This perspective makes the cross an even more amazing event. God wasn't only addressing our sin by providing a way for forgiveness and redemption; He was granting us access to His holiness. He provided a way for us to live with Him for all eternity. In light of this holiness, His love for us led to the obedience of the cross.

The Desert and Spilled Coffee
Like infinity, the holiness of God is also impossible to comprehend. But some flawed analogies at this point might be of some help.

Imagine that God is the Sahara Desert and that He is made up out of the trillions and trillions of grains of sand. He is pure and made up of only 100% sand and nothing else. If you were to add one grain of *salt* to this vast expanse of desert *sand*, God would cease to be pure, He would cease to be holy, untainted, and unstained. He would be contaminated (unholy) due to the presence of this one grain of salt.

Or try this one on for size: Noah is on the Ark one morning enjoying a cup of morning coffee when he accidently spills his mug off of the railing and into the surrounding ocean. At that moment, the world-encompassing ocean would cease to be a pure and undefiled body of water.

You may think that one cup of coffee gets watered down and blended into the ocean pretty well, and that the ocean on the other side of the planet is still pure and coffee-less. But technically, the ocean as a whole is now tainted and even impure; it is now contaminated (unholy) due to this one cup of spilled coffee.

God's holiness is like a desert without one grain of salt. God's holiness is like the oceans of the world without one cup of coffee added to their depths. When we say God is holy, we are saying a lot. God is not mostly holy or really, really holy; He is wholly holy.

The Holiness of God is Emphasized Throughout the Scriptures
When God spoke to Moses, the ground on which He appeared was holy ground. The tabernacle was set up as a holy place for Him to dwell as the Hebrew people traveled toward their Promised Land. Later the temple in Jerusalem was the home of the Holy One of Israel.

When Biblical writers wanted to make a point crystal clear to their readers, words were repeated to ensure that they had the reader's full attention. Christ Himself said, "Truly, truly I say unto you ..." in John 3:3 before He spoke truth to those He was teaching.

God is never referred to as "Almighty, Almighty, Almighty God." The Scriptures never point out that "God is Love, Love, Love." But in

Isaiah 6:3, the seraphim around God's throne cry out day and night, for all eternity, "Holy, Holy, Holy is the Lord Almighty!"

Holy is Not Something God *Does*

Holiness is an attribute that sets God apart from all created beings. It refers to His majesty and His perfect, moral purity. There is absolutely no sin or evil thought in God. His holiness is the very definition of that which is pure and righteous.

Holy is not what God does; it is the way He is. God does not conform to an outside standard; He is the very standard. He is holy and incomprehensibly pure. In fact, He is incapable of not being holy. It is the way He is. Because of this, His every attribute is also holy. When you think, "God," you must also think, "holy."[1]

God is holy, which means He is wholly not like us. We can strive to live righteous, pure, and holy lives, but even a newborn baby, whose only experiences in life include being born, spitting up, and cuddling in his mother's arms, is not a holy being; we are all unholy and impure at birth.

> "For all have sinned and fall short of the glory of God."
> (Romans 3:23)

We Live in a Broken-down House

The world in which we live is not the world that was created for us. Sin has cast a very long, dark shadow upon it. This makes it even harder for us to understand God's holiness because we live in a largely unholy place. We live in a fallen world amongst a fallen people.

Our current living situation is described quite well by Dr. Paul Tripp. He compares our current world to an old, broken-down, and dilapidated house that has been damaged by the effects of sin. Every room of this house has been marred. No part of it, not a single room in it, reflects the glory that was so evident when this house was first built. "Sin has left this world in a sorry condition. You see it everywhere you look."[2]

But because you and I were born into this broken-down house, this world is all we know. We see the continual unholiness that is all around us as the norm. We are largely desensitized to our current spiritual condition as people and as individuals. We are far too comfortable and undisturbed with the world in which we live because we rarely see ourselves the same way God sees us. "We have learned to live with unholiness and have come to look upon it as a natural and expected thing."[3]

But without recognizing the magnitude (and consequence) of our sin, we will never change. Without recognizing the magnitude of God's holiness, we will never truly be in awe of Him and motivated to change. We live our lives largely unaware of the severity of our current plight.

We never experience pure holiness. Because of this we have a much harder time fully understanding what holiness really is. We have nothing with which to accurately compare God. We cannot simply think of something that we think of as pure and then multiply that idea of purity a million times over. That idea of purity times a million is still not an accurate picture of God.[4]

The truth is, and will be for as long as we live in this broken-down house, we have little or no idea what divine holiness is really like. It's totally unique and incomprehensible to us. We are blinded to it. We can fear His power, we can admire His other attributes, but His holiness will always be something we will never fully – or even partially accurately grasp.

God's Holiness is Seen in His Actions

God is holy and set apart from us. This holiness makes Him transcendent and "other" than us. But fortunately, there's much more. There are huge implications of the fact that God is holy in His nature. Because God is holy, He is always righteous in His actions. He always does what is right; He never does anything wrong. He always acts in righteous ways with us because His very nature is holy.[5]

A God who is holy in His nature has no choice but to act holy in His interactions with us. It's not *part* of His character that He can choose to follow or not follow; it *is* His nature. God's actions are always holy because He *is* holy. God's holiness also reveals to us the attribute of His goodness.

We might not see or recognize His actions as holy or good on the receiving end; we must live by faith in that regard. When we trust that God allows everything to happen according to and for His holy and good purposes, only then do we recognize the holy hand of God in every situation.

> "And we know that in all things God works for the good
> of those who love Him, who have been called according to

22

His purpose. For those God foreknew He also predestined
to be conformed to the likeness of His Son…"
(Romans 8:28-29)

Believers are in the continual process of being refined into the likeness
of Christ (Romans 8:29). That is why no matter what our situation or
circumstances, we can say that every act of God in our lives is holy and
is designed to refine us and to make us more like the Holy One.

The Consequences and Implications of God's Holiness

God's holiness cannot tolerate forever the wrong and evil that is done
in this world. It may appear that sin has free reign and goes
unpunished, but God's holiness cannot allow for that.

"Your eyes are too pure to look on evil; You cannot tolerate wrong."
(Habakkuk 1:13)

The consequence of sin is death and eternal separation from God. The
holiness of God is much more than a "theory" for us to consider. His
holiness and our sin bring us death.

"For the wages of sin is death …"
(Romans 6:23)

God is righteous, and this means that He cannot ignore evil. It is
because of this righteousness that Christ Himself had to experience
God's wrath when our sins were placed on Him.

"Jesus cried out in a loud voice, 'My God,
My God, why have you forsaken Me?'"
(Matthew 27:45-46)

Sin and Broken Fellowship

This last passage is hard for us to read. Christ's crying out in anguish
because He has been forsaken by His Father is not an easy concept for
us to come to grips with. For many, it's a troubling statement.

Theologians debate its subtle nuances and argue over all that the
passage might really entail. But what everyone can agree on is this:
God took our sin very seriously when it was placed on Christ because
He takes His holiness very seriously.

Most believers live their entire lives never fully realizing the intensity
of the moment and the magnitude of what happened at the cross.
Every Easter we think about the physical pain of Christ's crucifixion,
but the broken fellowship Christ experienced on the cross was the
worst of all the pains He felt that day.

"As Jesus bore the guilt of our sins alone, God the Father, the mighty creator, the Lord of the universe, poured out on Jesus the fury of His wrath: Jesus became the object of the intense hatred of sin and vengeance against sin which God had patiently stored up since the beginning of the world."[6]

God takes His holiness seriously enough to pour out His wrath and His fury on His very own Son. This is why Jesus felt forsaken by His father.

Why Does God Take Sin So Seriously?

Why *does* God take His holiness and our sin so seriously? It's simply because God has made holiness the moral condition necessary for a healthy universe to exist, and sin is the disease that brings illness to His creation. Evil (unholiness) brings moral sickness to His world. This sickness then brings death.

God's first and foremost concern for His creation is its moral health. Sin brings spiritual disease to those created in His image, and in order to preserve His creation, He must destroy whatever would destroy it.[7] Evil is anything that is an offense to God, not just the "big ticket" sins we often think of.

How Do We Respond to God's Holiness?

Non-believers hope that if God does exist, His love and mercy will override His supposed holiness. Most people hope to be "good enough" to not lose their place in heaven because to them salvation is something that is *lost*, not something *gained* through forgiveness. This thought process happens in the minds of unbelievers a million times a day because they do not understand the holy nature of God.

Believers are not exempt from having a tainted view of God's holiness. Millions of professing Christians see God as "an indulgent old man, who Himself has no relish for folly, but leniently winks at the 'indiscretions of youth.'"[8] This view of God's reaction to our sin glosses over the passages of Scripture that show us the truth of our sin in light of His holiness.

> "The arrogant cannot stand in your presence;
> You hate all who do wrong."
> (Psalm 5:5)

Why "God is Holy" is a BIG DEAL

God's holiness provides a pattern for His people to imitate. Our theology determines our behavior. Those who are true disciples are willing to say, "I want to be holy because God is holy." Holy living is an expectation of those who believe. The Scriptures testify to this.

> "Be holy, because I am holy."
> (1 Peter 1:16)

> "Make every effort to live in peace with all men and to
> be holy; without holiness no one will see the Lord."
> (Hebrews 12:14)

Our religion is seen in what we do with our solitude. Our sin is preferring a passing pleasure to the fellowship that comes from obedience and sharing in His holiness. We don't desire holiness as much as we desire easiness. This is the battle we find ourselves fighting every day: the fight for holiness by imitating and reflecting God to others.

We are the temples in which God dwells. In the Old Testament, God's presence lived in the tabernacle that moved around with the wandering Hebrew people. In the New Testament, this sacred place was called the "Holy of Holies," found in the temple in Jerusalem. Where does God live now?

> "Don't you know that you yourselves are God's
> temple and that God's Spirit lives in you?"
> (1 Corinthians 3:16)

The answer is expounded upon with a call to live a spirit-filled life.

> "Be very careful, then, how you live – not as unwise but as
> wise, making the most of every opportunity, because the
> days are evil. Therefore do not be foolish, but understand
> what the Lord's will is. Do not get drunk on wine, which
> leads to debauchery. Instead, be filled with the Spirit."
> (Ephesians 5:15-18)

Can darkness dwell with light? Can God take pleasure in our filthy rags? The very best that we can present to God is still defiled and corrupt. God never asks us to do anything that is unreasonable. He never asks us to be omniscient or omnipotent, but He does ask us to be holy.

Holiness is more than avoiding sin. While living a holy life is a command for those who believe, it's also not the easiest thing to do.

Living a life that is holy and pleasing to God means more than just saying "no" to sin, it means saying "yes" to the things of God.

When I was a youth pastor, I would use an object lesson to drive this point home. I would give the kids an empty, plastic 2-liter bottle with the challenge to get all the air out. They were told the bottle represented them and the air inside represented all the sin in their lives.

They enjoyed the challenge. They would stomp on the bottle, sit on the bottle, and even try to suck all the air out of the bottle until they almost passed out. But no matter how hard they tried, there was always some air left inside.

Then I would pull out another 2-liter bottle filled completely with water. To live a holy life, you must do more than just say "no" to the things of the world; you must daily say "yes" to the things of God. You must daily seek Him and abide in Him. You must fill yourself with God's Spirit, not just avoid sinning.

This is the problem with many support groups that attempt to break sinful behavior without replacing it with something else. "Subtraction without addition leads to multiplication" is a common theme with those doing biblical counseling. Holy living is found in saying "yes" and not just in saying "no."

Holiness is good for us. Our personal holiness is not a prerequisite handed down by a morally demanding God; it is the means to and a source of blessing. Many think that following Christ means having less fun than living for yourself, but the truth is, blessings flow to those who live to imitate Christ.

There are huge blessings to be found by "seeking first the Kingdom of God and His righteousness" (Matthew 6:33). This is also seen when:

> "The eyes of the Lord range throughout the earth to strengthen
> those whose hearts are fully committed to Him."
> (2 Chronicles 16:9)

Holiness is God's gift that we receive by faith. When we are forgiven of our sins, we are found holy and acceptable to God. Salvation is a gift given to us because we are found holy in the sight of God. Our holiness is not found in living godly lives, but in declaring our ungodliness and casting its cost on Another. Your holiness has been enabled by Another – Christ Himself.

26

Sanctification is a big "churchy" word, the kind of word I had hoped to avoid using in this book. But here I must, because sanctification is the process of becoming more like Christ in our walk with God. In other words, sanctification is the lifelong process of our actions catching up to who and what we already are – a holy person.

As believers, we are filled with the Holy Spirit; this makes us holy beings. Having our actions match up with our spiritual standing is the lifelong journey in which we all find ourselves.

"You are a chosen people, a royal priesthood,
a holy nation, a people belonging to God…"
(1 Peter 2:9-10)

Reflection Questions:

1. What does it means to "share in His holiness" in Hebrews 12:10?
2. Are there activities or relationships in your life that you need to let go?
3. Do you see yourself as holy and acceptable to God? Why or why not?
4. Does a suspicion of holiness lie beneath your struggle to forsake your sinful actions? Explain.
5. Which do you desire more – holiness or easiness? What are the consequences of each?
6. Do you see holiness as something you must strive for or something you receive?
7. Because God is Holy, I will . . .

"Think-On-It" Verse:
"Our fathers disciplined us for a little while
as they thought best; but God disciplines us for
our good; that we may share in His holiness."
Hebrews 12:10

"But God demonstrates His own love for us in this:
While we were still sinners, Christ died for us."
Romans 5:8

3 - God is Loving

My Least Favorite Bible Verse

Many people have a favorite Bible verse. I do. But are we allowed to
have a least favorite verse? Is that against the rules? I know the Bible
is the inspired Word of God, and I don't mean to be disrespectful to
any part of it. But there is one verse that is my least favorite.

> "Whoever does not love does not
> know God, because God is love."
> (1 John 4:8)

Now you might be really confused or even a bit frustrated. Of all the
verses to choose from, why is this my least favorite? Before you toss
the book across the room in disgust, let me explain. It's the phrase at
the end that throws me: God is love. What does that even mean? Love
is a verb; it's something you do, not something you are.

God is Not Love?

The problem with the phrase, God is love, is that it is misinterpreted
by so many. When people read the verse, they assume that God is *only*
love, but that's not what John is saying.

Many hear "God is Love" and take it to mean that God, by *definition,* is
love. But John was *describing* God, not offering a definition. Tozer
articulated this much better.

> "If literally God is love, then literally love is God, and we are in all
> duty bound to worship love as the only God there is. If love is
> equal to God then God is only equal to love, and love and God
> are identical. Thus we destroy the concept of personality in God
> and deny outright all His attributes save one, and that one we
> substitute for God."[1]

God is *much more* than just love, and when the word *love* becomes His
definition and not just a *description* of Him, we have a seriously tainted
view of the Sovereign.

If God is *only* Love, He cannot be just. If God is *only* love, then there
are no consequences found in living lives to please only the flesh and
denying His call to repentance and holy living. Thankfully, God is

much more than only a God of love. He is also holy, just, faithful, and true. Love is just one attribute of God among many. God is a unity, which means He never puts an attribute on hold so He can then exercise another. He is always loving, even while He is acting justly by punishing sin.[2]

God is Loving

John was not saying with the phrase, "God is Love" that God is *only* love but that He is *always loving*. The Scriptures elsewhere say that God is just (2 Thessalonians 1:6), but no one sees the word *just* as an all-inclusive definition in the way that many see *love* as an all-inclusive definition.

We learn even more about God's love when we are reminded of all His other attributes. Because God is self-existent, His love has no beginning. Because God is eternal, His love has no end. Because God is holy, His love for us is pure. And because God is infinite, His love for us is limitless, incomprehensibly vast, and bottomless.[3]

Would You Die for Anyone?

The list of names of people I would die for is very, very short. And truth be told, if you bought a million copies of this book, your name still would not be added to the list. (You may become my new best friend, but my appreciation would end there). But if I had to, I would die for any one of my three children because I have a love for them that is impossible to fully describe.

I was raised in a great home, but I never knew how much I was loved as a kid until I became a parent. It was then, and only then, when I realized the love my parents have for me. God loves you with that same kind of love. He loves you as one of His children – even more than you love your children.

Many people have absent, painful, and broken relationships with their parents. For them, the thought of God as a loving Father may be a painful and almost cruel joke. It's difficult for many people to separate their human experience from the divine experience of a loving heavenly Father.

But the truth is, we all need to take great care to separate our earthly experiences with a faulty human father – to not let them affect the way we view our heavenly Father. The difference between them can never be measured. God is your loving "Abba Daddy" (Romans 8:15) while at the same time He is the mysterious and infinite God of all creation.

God's Love Separates the Christian Faith from Other Religions

All religions are not the same; there are huge differences among our faiths. The love God has for us is one of them. The God of the Bible is loving.

This is in huge contrast to the other gods of this world who are vengeful and in constant need of appeasement. The gods of other faiths are never satisfied; they are needy by nature and never content. In fact, even the material idols that we have set up for ourselves are never satisfied. Our desire for material things is never fulfilled, never fully satisfied.

God's Love is Self-Giving in Nature and for Others Benefit

This attribute shows that it is God's nature to give of Himself in order to bring about blessing and good for others. This also is seen to its fullest degree in the death of Christ. God loves to bless us because He Himself is glorified and honored by it.

"It is one of the most amazing facts in all Scripture that just as God's love involves His giving of Himself to make us happy, so we can in return give of ourselves and actually bring joy to God's heart."[4]

God's Love is Genuine and from His Heartfelt Concern for Us

God's love for us is seen in His passionate concern for our welfare. This is a great evidence of God's love for us. His concern for His creation shows a genuine love and concern for us. J. I. Packer writes:

"If a father continues cheerful and carefree while his son is getting into trouble, or if a husband remains unmoved when his wife is in distress, we wonder how much love is in their relationship, for we know that those who truly love are only happy when those whom they love are truly happy also."[5]

God's Love Seeks to Awaken a Responsive Love in Us for Him

God loves us enough to seek us out like a shepherd seeks his lost sheep. When Jesus walked among us, He loved us with compassion and mercy. He saw us as sheep without a shepherd. God loves us enough to suffer the humiliation of the cross for our redemption. Because of His self-giving love, He wills good, and not evil, for all of us.

5 Important Facts about God's Love

In his book, *The Attributes of God*, Arthur Pink did an excellent job of explaining several aspects of God's love. Here are five of them that are important for us to always remember.[6]

1. God's love is uninfluenced by our actions. There is nothing we can do to gain, lose, attract, or prompt God to love us more (or less) than He already does. His love is unique, not like the love we have for one another. We have a love that is often conditional, but God's love for us is unconditional, without merit or cause. It cannot be influenced by what we do or don't do.

What's so amazing about this uninfluenced love is that God chooses to love us in spite of our being so unlovable. We are diseased with sin and grossly depraved yet God loves us. We think mostly of ourselves and continually desire things that never satisfy. But the truth is, "We love Him, because He first loved us" (1 John 4:19). We did nothing to deserve His affection except to be His creation.

2. God's love is eternal because God Himself is eternal. God has no beginning; therefore, neither does His love. Like infinity, eternity is impossible to comprehend, but the scriptures tell us of God's eternal love for His people in Jeremiah 31:3, "I have loved you with an everlasting love…"

It's actually quite mind-boggling to think that God loved us even before our creation.

"For He chose us in Him before the creation of the world to be holy and
blameless in His sight. In love, He predestined us to be adopted as His
sons through Jesus Christ, in accordance with His pleasure and will."
(Ephesians 1:4-5)

Because God is infinite and eternal, His love for us is also infinite and eternal.

3. God's love is sovereign because He Himself is sovereign. God is under obligation to no one. He acts only according to His own pleasure, and it is His pleasure to love us. God does as He pleases – that *is* His job description. It's what He does. He has no choice in the matter. He cannot be influenced by anything in us or outside of us. He would cease to be God if He were not sovereign in His love for us.

Suppose for a moment that the opposite were true. Suppose God's love was ruled or regulated by something outside of Himself. If that were the case, He would love by rule, and loving by rule, He would be under a law of love, He would not be free, He would be beholden to follow the rules; and at that moment would cease to be God. He would then be something far less.

4. God's love is unchanging. God does not change (James 1:17), and because of this, God's love for us cannot grow or shrink. This truth is also seen by example in the final hours of Christ's life.

> "It was just before the Passover Feast. Jesus knew that the
> time had come for Him to leave this world and go to the
> Father. Having loved His own who were in the world,
> He now showed them the full extent of His love."
> (John 13:1)

Christ loved the disciples in a humble, self-sacrificing way, even though He knew one friend would soon betray Him, one would deny Him, and the others would be cowering in fear for their lives. God's love for us is undying, without condition, and inseparable from us (Romans 8:35-39).

5. God's love is holy and not ruled by shifting passions or feelings. God's love for us is pure and by principle.

> "And you have forgotten that word of encouragement that addresses
> you as sons: 'My son, do not make light of the Lord's discipline, and
> do not lose heart when He rebukes you, because the Lord disciplines
> those He loves, and He punishes everyone He accepts as a son.'"
> (Hebrews 12:5-6)

The love God has for us is holy and untainted. God cannot ignore sin, even in His own people. He loves us as we are, but He hates our sin. God alone is capable of truly "loving the sinner but hating the sin." He alone is able to separate who we *are* from what we *do*. He loves us as His children, but our sin can never be tolerated or embraced, even as He cradles us in His loving arms.

Why "God is Loving" is a BIG DEAL

Love and Fear: In many respects, we are driven mostly by our fears. Fear can be a good thing when it helps us to run away from danger. But fear is a bad thing when it robs us of our joy. God's desire is for us to be a people who live in peace, in fear of nothing, and with a sense of joy in all things.

> "There is no fear in love. But perfect love drives out
> fear, because fear has to do with punishment. The
> one who fears is not made perfect in love."
> (1 John 4:18)

Remembering God's love for us is our greatest weapon in our ongoing battle with fear. We have nothing to fear when this life is over.

Eternity with Him awaits all who believe and follow Him. We have nothing to fear in the present when we remember all that God's love means for us today.

Love and Trust: God is worthy of our trust when we realize His love for us. Having a faith in God is often easier than actually trusting Him for the details of our lives. It's ironic that we often believe God has done the most amazing miracles in the Bible, and we believe He can do anything He desires, but we fail to trust Him with our daily needs and concerns.

We are not asked to put our trust in some impersonal force like a Star Wars character. We are asked to put our trust in a God who loves each of us as individuals. We are asked to trust a God who loves us in a sacrificial way. We are asked to trust in a God who loves us only because it pleases Him to do so.

Love and Rest: Our hearts should find rest knowing that God's love for us is eternal, without a beginning or an end. Our minds should be at peace when we realize that God loved us first with an undeserved love: "We love Him, because He first loved us" (1 John 4:19). God does not love us because we loved Him first. If indeed God did love only in response to our love for Him, then it would not be unmerited on His part. Furthermore, rest and reassurance are found when we realize that nothing can separate the believer from God's love (Psalm 136:1; Romans 8:38-39).

Regardless of your circumstances, know that God loves you. God loves His Son but also allowed Him to be spat upon. We can never call into question God's love for us because of our experiences. Christ did not walk an easy road. He often had no place to rest. He suffered. He was humiliated and experienced the pain and shame of death on a cross. Our love for God cannot depend on our circumstances.

Love and Service: Because God's love is self-giving in nature, we need to make our love and service to others a fruit that is easily evident in our lives.

> "We imitate this communicable attribute of God, first by loving God in return, and second by loving others in imitation of the way God loves them."[7]

This encouragement to be a people who not only receive God's love but who give it back in return is seen in the words of Christ Himself:

> "Love the Lord your God with all your heart and with all your soul

and with all your mind. This is the first and greatest commandment.
And the second is like it: Love your neighbor as yourself."
(Matthew 22:37-39)

Love and Covenant: God's love for us allows us to love and enjoy Him in a covenant relationship.

> "A covenant relation is one in which two parties are permanently pledged to each other in mutual service and dependence."[8]

A *contract* relationship is made for a limited period of time, is based on an "if-then" mentality, deals with specific actions, and is motivated to get something we want.

But a *covenant* relationship is a permanent commitment, made with unconditional promises, based on steadfast love, for the benefit of the other person, and at times requires confrontation and forgiveness.

We are pledged to Him, and He is pledged to us. We do not have a contract that can expire or later be renegotiated. We have a life-long partnership with the living God that is not easily broken.

Reflection Questions:

1. Why might the phrase, "God is not love" be troubling to people?
2. What happens if God is *only* love and nothing else?
3. What would you say to someone who feels like God does not love them?
4. Is your love for God unconditional or based on your circumstances?
5. What does it mean that God loves you with an infinite, unconditional love?
6. Why do we feel the need to continually please God in order to keep His love?
7. Because God is loving, I will . . .

"Think-On-It" Verse:

"For God so loved the world that He gave His one and only Son, that whoever believes in Him shall not perish but have eternal life. For God did not send His Son into the world to condemn the world, but to save the world through Him."
John 3:16-17

"Have mercy on me, O God, according to Your unfailing love;
according to Your great compassion blot out my transgressions.
Wash away all my iniquity and cleanse me from my sin."
Psalm 51:1-2

4 - God is Merciful

(God does NOT give us what we deserve.)

The Princess and the Monster

On August 31, 1997, Princess Diana was killed in a car accident. On November 28, 1994, Jeffrey Dahmer was killed in prison while serving multiple life sentences for killing 16 people. Princess Diana was an actual Princess. She was pretty, elegant, and had two young sons. She did a lot of great charitable work, was adored by millions, and was well respected by the entire world. Jeffrey Dahmer raped and killed young boys and then cannibalized portions of their bodies.

According to reports, before Jeffrey Dahmer died, he gave his life to Christ and became a born-again believer. I don't know what Princess Diana believed in her heart about the person of Christ and His redemptive work of the cross. If the reports are true, on November 28, 1994, Jeffrey Dahmer went to heaven. If Princess Diana never asked Christ to forgive her of her sins, then on August 31, 1997, she did not.

Radical Mercy

This very thought is either offensive or absurd to most people. This kind of mercy is impossible for the world to understand, but it's also hard for many Christians to believe as well. When we cannot understand how something like this could happen, it's because we don't understand God's mercy.

Mercy is God NOT giving us what we really do deserve. We think of Jeffrey Dahmer as a monster who deserved to go to hell. On the contrary, Princess Diana was a good person who deserved to go to heaven. In this respect, "life is not fair." Praise God.

Mercy is the attribute of God which moves Him to be actively compassionate with divine pity. Since God's justice is satisfied in the death and resurrection of Jesus, He is free to show mercy to all those who have chosen to follow Him. Like everything else about God, it is also found in eternal measure and will never end since it is a part of God's infinite nature.[1]

Mercy and Grace Confusion

Mercy and Grace are often confused. They have similar aspects but are not the same.

Mercy is … God *not punishing* us as our sins deserve.

Grace is … God *blessing us* despite the fact that we do not deserve it.

Mercy is … God *withholding* judgment.

Grace is … God *giving kindness* to the unworthy.

Mercy and grace are best illustrated in the salvation that is available through Christ. We deserve judgment, but when we receive Jesus as our Savior, we receive mercy from God, and we are delivered from judgment. Instead of judgment, by grace we receive salvation, forgiveness of sins, abundant life, and an eternity with Him.

What Rights Do We Really Have?

We often fall into the trap of assuming that we have certain rights, most which we really don't have at all. Recently the Wal-Mart near our home was remodeled and reorganized. When the work was finished, a lot of items were in new and different places. I was amazed at the anger I saw in people as they tried to find their items, fill their carts, and check things off their lists. I really believe many thought, "Wal-Mart has no right to move my spaghetti sauce aisle!"

My perspective was just the opposite: it's their store; they can do anything they want to with it. They can sell spaghetti sauce from the rooftop if they'd like. I can't go into someone else's home and demand they move their furniture around. We don't have the right to tell Wal-Mart where to put their spaghetti sauce.

If God wants to show mercy to Jeffrey Dahmer, it's His right to do so. "I will have mercy on whom I have mercy, and I will have compassion on whom I have compassion." This vitally important point is actually made twice, word for word, in both the Old Testament (Exodus 33:19) and the New Testament (Romans 9:15). It's God's world; He can run it as He pleases.

Our Response to Mercy

Instead of complaining that God shows mercy to the worst of sinners, the reality is that we should simply rejoice that God shows mercy to anyone at all. Because of the mercy of God, our response should be to fall on our knees in worship and thanksgiving.

> "I love the Lord, for He heard my voice;
> He heard my cry for mercy."
> (Psalm 116:1)

Many see the God of the Old Testament as a God of justice, wrath, and vengeance while the New Testament picture of Him is one of mercy, grace, and forgiveness. This is not at all accurate. We are terribly mistaken if we think "Old Testament God" was a God of judgment while "New Testament God" was a God of mercy and grace. There is no difference between the two.

While the New Testament does give us a fuller picture of redemptive truth, the exact same God spoke to both ages. Whenever He spoke, He always acted like Himself, whether in the Garden of Eden or the Garden of Gethsemane. He has always been merciful, and He has always been just.[2]

Mercy is Not a Mood
God is unchanging. This means that mercy is not a mood that comes and goes with God. We do not receive mercy if we catch Him on a good day. We do not receive justice if we catch Him in "one of His moods." Like God Himself, mercy has no beginning, and it will have no end. God's mercy is never-ending.

Mercy is Not Shown to Every Creature
God has never extended mercy to the angels because they have never needed it. They have never sinned or come under the effects of the curse. But God has extended grace to them. He elected them to be angels and sovereignly preserved them from the fall of Satan.[3]

Mercy is Temporary for Some
Mercy that God shows to non-believers is temporary and is confined only to this present life. There will be no mercy extended to them beyond the grave. Mercy is eternal, but it is seen differently in the lives of believers and non-believers. God shows a certain amount of mercy to everyone. General mercy is extended to all of God's creation.

"The Lord is good to all, and His mercies are over all His works."
(Psalm 145:9)

God's mercy allows even the ungodly to accomplish amazing things, but His mercy for those who do not believe ends on this earth.[4]

Mercy is and Always has Been Present
God can never cease to be merciful; it is His divine nature. He does not turn it on and off; it's always on. But the exercise of His mercy is regulated by His divine will; nothing obliges Him to act. If anything outside of God obliged Him to act, He would not be supreme and would cease to be God.[5]

God would still be merciful even without the presence of sin. Although it would be hidden and unknown to us, it would still be there because it is a part of His eternal character. Our sin and the fall of man are what allow mercy to be active and at work in this world.[6]

Mercy is for Those Who are in Trouble

In the Scriptures, mercy is most often seen when people are in misery and distress – when they have a need to be rescued. The same is true for us today, God's mercy is seen when we have a need.[7]

God not only shows mercy on us when we are in trouble; His mercy extends far beyond that. His mercy rescues us from the misery and distress of our sin. As Adam's fallen children, we are all in trouble. We are all in need of rescue. We are all in need of God's mercy.

Mercy is Not Leniency

God is merciful, not lenient. Never confuse the two. God hates sin. He abhors what Jeffrey Dahmer did. He chooses to show mercy where and when He desires, but He is never okay with our sin.

Why "God is Merciful" is a BIG DEAL

In order to receive mercy, we must first know that God is merciful. We cannot have access to it – we cannot receive it – if we do not know that God is the source.[8]   If you see God as unmerciful, He will oblige that notion. He gives mercy to those who humbly seek it as a part of His infinite nature. Our pride is often a deterrent to our receiving all of God's gifts.

Without God's mercy, we are all lost for eternity. Because God has chosen to show us mercy, we should be in a continual state of praise. Mercy should put a perpetual grin on our faces that only a plastic surgeon could remove. We have a guarantee that our salvation is a lasting promise.

> "In His great mercy He has given us new birth into a living
> hope through the resurrection of Jesus Christ from the dead,
> and into an inheritance that can never perish, spoil or fade."
> (1 Peter 1:3-4)

Mercy should put a bounce in our step every day. Celebrating the mercy of God is a major theme of the Psalms. God's mercy toward us should be the fuel of our praise, adoration, and celebration of who we are in Him. His mercy needs to be remembered far more often then it is, and appreciated daily by those who benefit from it.

Because God is infinite and merciful, we can keep coming back to Him without fear. You can never wear out or exhaust God's patience. Christ told us to forgive "70 times 7" those who offend us. God is a forever-forgiving God because of His unending mercy.

"Let us then approach the throne of grace with confidence, so that we may receive mercy and find grace to help us in our time of need."
(Hebrews 4:16)

Mercy is also something we extend to others. Loving our enemies and treating them well is as absurd to the world as Princess Diana not going to heaven. We honor God, and we imitate His merciful will by treating others better than they deserve. But the deeper truth is, those who fail to extend mercy to others are demonstrating that they really have no idea what they are being saved from.

God extends more mercy to the merciful. God cares for our needs and shows us mercy regardless of our level of compassion for others, but when we show this quality toward others – when we show mercy God more readily and more demonstrably shows mercy toward us.

"Blessed is he who has regard for the weak;
the Lord blesses him in times of trouble."
(Psalm 41:1)

Mercy brings perspective. When we truly understand God's mercy for us, we grieve over our sin. We genuinely repent, and we never again have the audacity to approach Him with a sense of entitlement. Mercy makes us realize that all we have is an undeserved gift.

Reflection Questions:

1. Why do we have a hard time extending mercy to others?
2. What do we really deserve from God?
3. Why do we think we have certain rights?
4. Do you ever wonder if you will exhaust God's mercy with your continual sin and repentance?
5. Do you see God as merciful or lenient? What is the difference?
6. How are grieving over your sin and receiving mercy related?
7. Because God is merciful, I will . . .

"Think-On-It" Verse:
"Give thanks to the Lord, for He is good!
For His mercy endures forever."
Psalm 136:1

> "For the law was given through Moses; grace
> and truth came through Jesus Christ."
> John 1:17

5 - God is Gracious
(God gives us what we do NOT deserve.)

A Great King James Word

Grace is God giving us what we do not deserve. It is His goodness
directed at our debt. Grace is what we call it when God imparts or
imputes His righteousness into us.

As a kid, I grew up with the New American Standard translation of the
Bible. Then one day at church they trotted out the New International
Version Bibles. Now I had already memorized some verses in the
older version, and as hard as I try, I cannot re-memorize them in the
newer one.

So in Jeremiah 29:11, God has promised *me* "plans for welfare and not
for calamity" to give me "a future and a hope." But for my NIV kids,
in that very same verse, God has promised *them* "plans to prosper ...
and not to harm" to give them a "hope and a future." It pretty much
works out the same either way.

Now the King James Bible, that's another story. I get lost and
somewhat confused in the *thee's* and *thou's* and all that fancy Old-
English talk, but there is a word used in the King James Version that I
especially like – the word *impute*. In Romans 4, this word *impute* is used
six times:

⁶ God *imputeth* righteousness;
⁸ The Lord will not *impute* sin;
¹¹ Righteousness might be *imputed* unto them;
²² And therefore it was *imputed* to him for righteousness;
²³ Now it was not written for his sake alone, that it was *imputed* to him;
²⁴ To whom it shall be *imputed*, if we believe on Him that raised up Jesus

It's a great word because it captures a great truth. God "imputeth" His
righteousness to us. He gives *us* credit for something that *His Son*
accomplished on the cross. We are made righteous by the act of
Another. That's grace – pure and simple.

Grace and Mercy Confusion

Grace and mercy are often confused. Tozer had some clarifying thoughts on how they differ and how they work together:

> "In God, mercy and grace are one; but as they reach us they are seen as two, related but not identical. As mercy is God's goodness confronting human misery and guilt, so grace is His goodness directed toward human debt and demerit. It is by grace that God imputes merit where none existed and declares no debt to be where one had one before. Grace is the good pleasure of God that inclines Him to bestow benefits upon the undeserving."[1]

God enjoys giving great gifts to those who love Him, even when they do not deserve it. Grace is the way we describe that inclination. Jesus Christ is the channel through which His grace moves. When you hear the word *grace* think "Jesus" because He is the ultimate gift of grace given to us by the Father. The very source of Christian morality is the love of Christ, and not the law of Moses.[2]

> "For the law was given through Moses; grace
> and truth came through Jesus Christ."
> (John 1:17)

Without Jesus, the mercy God has on us would not be seen in His grace.

> "For if by the trespass of the one man, death reigned through
> that one man, how much more will those who receive God's
> abundant provision of grace and of the gift of righteousness
> reign in life through the one man, Jesus Christ."
> (Romans 5:17)

Even knowing this, we need to fully realize that grace is an eternal attribute of God. Grace existed before Christ took on flesh and walked as a man among us. Grace is unbounded and eternal. That is why where sin abounds, grace can be seen in even greater measure.[3]

We deserve nothing from God; He owes us nothing. Anything good that we experience is a result of the mercy and grace of God (Ephesians 2:5). Grace is simply His unmerited favor. God gives us good things that we do not deserve and could never earn. Arthur Pink defined grace this way:

> "Divine grace is the sovereign and saving favor of God exercised in the bestowment of blessings upon those who have no merit *in* them and for which no compensation is demanded *from* them."[4]

Saving Grace

In *Knowing God*, J.I. Packer writes, "Grace and salvation belong together as cause and effect."[5] This is attested to in Titus 2:11, "For the grace of God that brings salvation has appeared to all men" and in Ephesians 1:7, "In Him we have redemption through His blood, the forgiveness of sins, in accordance with the riches of God's grace." God's grace allows our salvation to become a reality.

Continual Grace

But grace is not just a one-time salvation thing. God continues to show us grace throughout our lives. Paul continually spoke of God's grace in His everyday life and ministry.

> "But by the grace of God I am what I am, and His grace to
> me was not without effect. No, I worked harder than all of
> them yet not I, but the grace of God that was with me."
> (1 Corinthians 15:10)

Grace is also a *continual acting* of God in our lives to enable us in our service and imitation of Him.

> "We have different gifts, according to the grace given to each of us.
> If your gift is prophesying, then prophesy in accordance with your
> faith; if it is serving, then serve; if it is teaching, then teach."
> (Romans 12:6-7)

Common Grace

Grace is also shown to all of us in general, non-specific ways. God's grace allows life, peace, and prosperity to all the inhabitants of His earth. These are the graces of God by which He gives blessings that are <u>not</u> a part of salvation:

Physical Grace: The rain falls on the just and the unjust. Both the good and the evil can prosper. Godless people can makes millions of dollars and live long, healthy lives because of God's grace.

Intellectual Grace: Even those with depraved minds can grasp truth and have great intelligence. People with absolutely no interest in God can design space shuttles and put men on the moon.

Moral Grace: God restrains people from living lives of pure evil. We do have the ability to live morally. As corrupt and sinful as this world is, it can be worse – and in fact, often has been.

Creative Grace: God gives gifts and abilities to whoever He chooses in the areas of music, art, literature, etc. Unfortunately, these God-given talents are often used to promote the worst of ungodly values.

Social Grace: We have order, organizations, families, government, and societal structure. We do have wars, conflict, and tension, but we also live in peace and tranquility with each other more than we realize.

Eternal, Free and Sovereignly Given

Arthur Pink went on to make these three additional important points about grace. First, grace is eternal in that it was planned before it was exercised in the Person and work of Christ. This is seen in the promise made only minutes after The Fall that One would come to crush the head of Satan (Genesis 3:15). Secondly, grace is free and cannot be earned. This goes against our human nature which senses that nothing this good is free. Third, grace is given sovereignly by God. He can give it to whoever He wishes.[6]

Is Grace Fair?

Grace is often seen by many as unfair, but to complain about this perceived partiality and unfairness is akin to the clay rising up against the potter and demanding an answer to, "why have you made me this way?" It is not our place to call into question the justice of the Divine.[7]

This supposed unfairness will be explained in more detail when we discuss the attribute of the righteousness of God. Until then, realize that God is gracious, and this grace includes His goodness, kindness, mercy, and love. If it were not for God's grace, His holiness would exclude us all from His eternal presence.

Thankfully, this is not the case, for He desires to know each of us personally, and He desires that none should perish.

> "This is good, and pleases God our Savior, who wants all men to be saved and to come to a knowledge of the truth."
> (1 Timothy 2:4)

Grace and the Quid Pro Quo

Quid pro quo is a Latin legal term meaning "what for what." It indicates an exchange (or substitution) of goods or services. We use the term to mean, "If you scratch my back, I'll scratch yours." Without realizing it, we often view our relationship with God in this way. We assume we live with the arrangement, "If we obey, He will bless."

Unfortunately, this mindset is most often revealed in us when trials come. When hard times come crushing down upon you, do you feel that God is not holding up His end of the deal? Do you feel that He is being unfair and letting you down? These thoughts may indicate a lack of a proper understanding of His grace.

When we think we have the right to a long, healthy, prosperous life because we go to church and obey God's commands, we do not have a proper understanding of His grace. We deserve nothing! Actually, that's not true either; we deserve death. Anything else we have or receive in this life is only due to the grace of God.

Grace is a Scary Thing

If grace is nothing but a good thing, why would anyone be afraid? How can grace be described as scary? Because if God is a God of grace who gives us what is not deserved, then we have a God who in reality has put everyone into His debt. God owes us nothing; we in turn owe Him everything.

The reason religion is so popular is because with religion we are the ones in charge. We can worship and serve as we desire. We sense that we can earn God's goodness and favor. We want a God who owes us something when we are obedient; that way we then have some control. But if God's favor cannot be earned – if it truly is a matter of grace – then we are not the ones in charge. God is.

Taxpayers have rights; we do not. When you pay taxes, you have a right to say how the money is spent. But when grace is a gift freely given, you do not have the right to insist how and to whom it is given. That is why grace is a scary thing to many – because now we have no rights. Grace leaves us without any leverage with God and having no bargaining position with God is a scary thing to many people.[8] He now can ask anything He likes of us. He owes us nothing, and we owe Him everything.

Grace is a Hard Thing

Grace is not an easy thing to accept and fully understand. We all have a knowledge deep within us that we are morally corrupt and in need of being saved. This corruption makes it hard to accept God's mercy and grace. We continually feel like we must *do something* to earn and keep God's favor. This is the trapping of the law.

The law says *"do"* but grace says *"done."* The law says we work to gain and keep favor, but grace says favor was given to us at the cross. This is unnatural to us. We think we have a right to receive what we have when we do right by following the law, rather than realize it is God's right to give as He wishes. When we obey the rules, we think we deserve God's goodness and blessing; but the truth is, we live and work *from* grace – not *for* grace.

44

We must live with a cross-centered understanding. God's righteous judgment against us would have been fair and just, but God showed us grace instead.

Why "God is Gracious" is a BIG DEAL

God extends grace to us; our job is to accept it as a free, unearned gift. There is only one way to receive grace, and that is through faith. Faith means depending upon another to do something you cannot do. It means accepting the fact that you can do nothing to attain righteousness by your own effort. When God's favor comes to us apart from our own merit, it must come on the merit of Another (that is, the Person of Jesus Christ).[9] We are to simply believe and accept what is freely given to us.

Grace is a lifelong gift. Grace is not just a one-time thing; it has to do with more than just our salvation. God continues to show us grace throughout our entire lives. Paul wrote, "By the grace of God I am what I am" (1 Corinthians 15:10). The New Testament writers saw the success of their ministry as dependent upon God's continuing grace.[10]

Grace is not just a one-time gift, but a continual acting of God in our lives to enable us in our service and reflection of Him. We should be "squatters at the throne of grace" each and every day. Park yourself there and stay – enjoy God's grace for the gift that it is.

God's continual grace is also there to help us specifically in our difficult times. Remember this truth: "God's grace is up to the challenge." No matter what your trials or difficult circumstances are, God's grace is bigger than the issues you are facing.

Grace is something we receive and extend. If God is willing to give us things that we don't deserve, we should be willing and able to do the same with others. Imitating Christ means living a life full of both grace and mercy for those around us. Showing grace in a world where it is often found in short supply is a powerful witness to those who experience it firsthand.

Everyone wants grace from others when they make a mistake or say something hurtful. We often even *expect* it from others when we are the ones who have committed the offense, but when someone has wronged us, it's often a very different story. The challenge is to extend grace freely to those who have hurt us or continually frustrate us. Grace is seen in our forgiveness of others.

Grace is what makes us different from the world. What makes you different from your neighbor? Or, for that matter, what makes you different from a rapist, murderer, or genocidal dictator? Do you think you deserve all that you have? Do you think you have earned all that you have accomplished and the benefits that have followed?

If you have ever shared the Gospel with someone who just didn't seem to get it, you have met someone with an unenlightened mind. If you know people who continually reject God's truth, you know people who have not been shown the grace of God to understand their sin and the way of redemption.

> "The god of this age has blinded the minds of unbelievers, so that
> they cannot see the light of the gospel of the glory of Christ, who
> is the image of God. For God, who said, 'Let light shine out of
> darkness,' made His light shine in our hearts to give us the light
> of the knowledge of the glory of God in the face of Christ."
> (2 Corinthians 4:4, 6)

You know all that you know because God allows you to know it. You have all that you have because God has given it to you. God made you who and what you are. His grace enables you to hear and to grasp His truth. The "foolishness" of the cross only makes sense to you because of His grace. As a result, we can never feel superior to those who fail to acknowledge His truth. We have no reason or ability to boast because it is only by God's grace that we recognize Christ as Savior.

Paul wrote about this in his letter to the Corinthians:

> "For who makes you different from anyone else? What do
> you have that you did not receive? And if you did receive
> it, why do you boast as though you did not?"
> (1 Corinthians 4:7)

"There but for the grace of God go I" is an old and worn out saying, but please don't let the triteness of this expression cause you to miss the point: it is only by God's grace that you know what you know, have what you have, and are what you are.

God reserves the right to give wisdom and insight to whomever He desires. Of the ostrich God says:

> "She lays her eggs on the ground and lets them warm in the sand,
> unmindful that a foot may crush them, that some wild animal may
> trample them. She treats her young harshly, as if they were not
> hers; she cares not that her labor was in vain, for God did not
> endow her with wisdom or give her a share of good sense."
> (Job 39:14-17)

46

Grace leaves us grateful, humble and worshipful. In his sermon on humility, Charles Spurgeon wrote of our spiritual enlightenment and the gratitude that is seen in our lives when we truly recognize God's grace as the cause of our understanding:

> "Never trace the difference between yourself and others to your own free will, nor to any betterness of your natural disposition, but entirely to the mercy and Grace of God which have been freely bestowed on you! Let Grace be magnified by your grateful heart!"[11]

When we truly recognize the full extent of God's grace sovereignly shown to us, we are both humbled and awed by His goodness to us. This awe leaves us with a worshipping heart, regardless of our present circumstances. We also then have no sense of entitlement because we go to church, teach a Sunday school class, or tithe.

The only proper response to God's grace is a heart of gratitude, with daily and sincere praise.

Reflection Questions:

1. Why do we fail to recognize the righteousness that has been "imputed" into us?
2. As you read your Bible, are you more aware of your sin or God's grace? Why?
3. Why is it so hard to accept God's grace as a free gift?
4. What would God be like without this attribute?
5. Why do we want to keep a measure of control over God?
6. What does it say about us when we think God is being unfair?
7. Because God is gracious, I will . . .

"Think-On-It" Verse:

"For it is by grace you have been saved, through faith,
and this not from yourselves, it is the gift of God."
Ephesians 2:8

"He is the Rock, His works are perfect, and all His ways are just.
A faithful God who does no wrong, upright and just is He."
Deuteronomy 32:4

6 - God is Righteous
(God is right in all He does.)

The Simpsons and Sunday School
The Simpsons TV show has had a huge impact on American culture. There are a lot of things not to like about the Simpsons, but they are one of the only television families that regularly attend church together. Here is a very insightful interchange Bart once had with his Sunday school teacher on the topic of hell:[1]

Miss Allbright: Today's topic will be hell.

Kids: Ooh.

Bart: All right. I sat through Mercy and I sat through Forgiveness. Finally, we get to the good stuff!

M.A.: Hell is a terrible place. Maggots are your sheet; worms, your blanket. There's a lake of fire burning with sulfur. You'll be tormented day and night, forever and ever. As a matter of fact, if you actually saw Hell, you'd be so frightened, you would die.

Bart: [raises his hand] Oh, Miss Allbright?

M.A.: Yes, Bart.

Bart: Wouldn't you eventually get used to it, like in a hot tub?

M.A.: No.

Bart: [raises his hand]

M.A.: Yes, Bart.

Bart: Are there pirates in hell?

M.A.: Yes. Thousands of them.

Bart: [rubs hands] Hoo hoo, baby!

Miss Allbright goes on to say that to avoid eternal damnation, you must obey the Ten Commandments. The plot then involves Lisa's fear that her dad Homer is going to hell because he's breaking one of the commandments by stealing free cable TV at home.

The Simpsons' Theology
First off, there is some tragically flawed theology in The Simpsons. Contrary to popular opinion, our salvation is *not* based on obeying the Ten Commandments.

Secondly, millions of people *do* think their salvation is based on obeying the Ten Commandments because millions of people base their theology and views of God on movies and TV shows like this one and others.

Third, Bart was bored by the topics of mercy and forgiveness. He sat through weeks of lessons of no interest to him, and now the payoff has finally arrived! He can finally hear about hell – the torment, the burning flames, and even the pirates. But the point is this: hell has become a joke and a punch line – something funny to laugh about. There is not a lot of fear these days of a righteous and just God. The notion of God's wrath is flat-out denied by most, and a source of entertainment to many others.

What to Call this Attribute?
Considerable thought went into how to title this attribute. Among the options were "God is Righteous," "God is Just," and "God is Wrathful." Even "God is Fair" was given some consideration.

The word *wrath* is a complicated word. It's laden with some pretty ugly connotations: anger, hate, and disgust, to name a few. We are told that God has wrath toward our sin, but it does not seem to fit with His character. God is fair in His dealings with us; but again, the word *fair* doesn't seem appropriate either; because it really doesn't properly convey God's attitude toward sin.

In the Bible, it seems the words *justice* and *righteous* are scarcely distinguished from each other. The same word in the original language becomes either *justice* or *righteousness* on a whim of the translator.[2]

The English language has different definitions for each word. For us, the word *righteous* means doing what is right while *justice* implies that some form of punishment is in the offering. The original authors and readers did not make the same distinction as we do today. They saw one definition, not two. They saw God as always doing what was right, just, correct, and fair.

But we still need a better idea of what "God is righteous and just" means. Wayne Grudem defines it this way: "God's righteousness means that God always acts in accordance with what is right and is Himself the final standard of what is right."[3]

Long before this definition was given, Moses described a righteous and just God this way:

49

"He is the Rock, His works are perfect, and all His ways are just.
A faithful God who does no wrong, upright and just is He."
(Deuteronomy 32:4)

The Way God Is – NOT Something He Does

You may be tempted to think that God is *required* to act when He witnesses something that is obviously wicked and sinful. We conclude that when God looked down on Sodom and Gomorrah; that He *had* to do *something* to punish the sin He saw before Him. But this view also shows that we may have a tainted view of God's righteousness. He is not required to do anything.

There is no standard or call to justice outside of God that requires Him to act or compels Him to intercede when He is confronted with evil. If there were, that would mean there are rules outside of God that He must follow. There are no principles that God must follow or be accountable to in this regard. There is nothing outside of Him that forces Him to act in any degree. All of His reasons for acting and interceding come from within. He does not – He cannot – change, so when we say that God is just, we are saying this is the way He IS; not that it is something He does. When He acts justly, He is not conforming to a predetermined criteria; He is simply acting like Himself.[4]

Conversely, everything that is good in this world is only good to the degree to which it conforms to the nature of God. Obviously, our sin (and evil itself) fails to conform to the nature of God in drastic ways. God is His own principle of rightness and fairness. When He acts to either punish evil or reward righteousness, He is simply acting like Himself, uninfluenced by anything that is outside of Himself.[5]

No On/Off Switch

Like mercy, God does not turn His justice on and off according to His mood or the events that He is witnessing. God is One – not a bunch of independent parts all working together as one entity. He is both merciful and just all the time. God is not a judge who reluctantly passes out judgments with mixed emotions or with a tear in His eye.

No Battle Within

God's attributes of mercy, love, forgiveness, holiness, and justice are all always working together, and they are never in conflict with one another. There is no battle within God where mercy and justice compete for the upper hand. If mercy wins, forgiveness is granted, and grace is awarded to the sinner. If justice wins, hell awaits that very same sinner – literally. This is not how God operates. When grace appears, justice is not violated, but is satisfied when God spares a sinner.[6]

No Apologies
Arthur Pink was a pastor – not just a theologian who wrote his high and lofty thoughts about God. When he wrote and spoke of God's wrath, it was to people he knew, saw, and interacted with in his own congregation regularly. He did not write about God's wrath as just a theory to consider. He was not just a detached scholar who could write on a difficult topic such as this and never have to face his audience.

Why bring this up? Because hell is a topic that is much easier to talk about in a seminary classroom than it is in the presence of those who may find themselves there when this life is over. A pastor who is willing to talk about God's wrath, as well as His love and forgiveness, is a leader who teaches what people need to hear instead of what they may want to hear.

No Hiding
God makes no attempts to hide His anger (His wrath) in the Scriptures. He never tries to conceal it; He is not ashamed one bit that vengeance and fury belong to Him.

> "See now that I myself am He! There is no god besides Me. I
> put to death and I bring to life, I have wounded and I will heal,
> and no one can deliver out of My hand. I lift My hand to heaven
> and declare: As surely as I live forever, when I sharpen my flashing
> sword and My hand grasps it in judgment, I will take vengeance
> on My adversaries and repay those who hate Me."
> (Deuteronomy 32:39-41)

The cross of Christ was necessary because God is both holy and just. Because God is holy, He cannot condone sin. Because God is just, He cannot ignore it either. God does not hide His anger by ignoring sin's existence.

No Blemish
God's righteousness is as much of His divine character as the more favored ones that we get so excited about – like His forgiveness, mercy, grace, love, and patience. Many fully embrace these more favored characteristics of God, but deny this one altogether. It's seen by millions of people as some sort of moral blemish that we have no choice but to begrudgingly accept as part of His package. We believe God is righteous and just, but we're not all that happy about it.

In reality, ignoring sin or being indifferent to evil would actually be a moral blemish on God's character.[7] Think about it for a moment. How could the same God who loves holiness, purity, and the beauty of innocence tolerate sin and all kinds of evil? How could God view in the same way both virtue and vice? Both wisdom and folly? How could God embrace by His tacit acceptance an ounce of darkness when He is a brilliant Light? How could He delight in the pure and not loathe what is vile? The very nature of God and life itself makes hell as much of a necessity as is heaven.[8]

No Embarrassment

When we fully understand the righteousness and justice of God, we have no need to be embarrassed because we actually believe in a place of eternal separation from God – a place of lasting punishment. It may grieve us that many have and will go there, but it's nothing that we should be hesitant or even ashamed to admit that we believe in.

Hell is not a popular topic these days; it never has been. It's something we don't talk about much because we don't want to be seen as one of those radical types who scream about hell when trying to scare someone into heaven. But if you believe in God, you believe in hell, and maybe it's something we should talk about more than we do.

No Defending

Not only does God make no effort to conceal His anger or wrath, He makes no effort to defend it. This goes back to the very definition of the righteousness of God. As Grudem explains:

"... we may ask what is right. In other words, what *ought* to happen and what *ought* to be. Here we must respond that *whatever conforms to God's moral character is right*. But why is whatever conforms to God's moral character right? It is right because it conforms to God's moral character."[9]

God is the one and only final standard of what is right and what is wrong, and He feels no need to defend this standard.

Job learned this lesson in an up close and personal conversation with God Himself. Job bitterly protested and complained that he had been treated unfairly and unjustly by God. Few of us would argue that Job did not have a strong case. But when Job finally did get his day in court before the Supreme Judge of all judges, God felt no need to defend Himself and His so-called unjust actions.

God didn't take the time to explain why He allowed all of this calamity to happen to Job. He only answered with a not-so-subtle statement of His own power, majesty, sovereignty, and right to act as He desires. He felt no need to explain the "rightness" of His actions. He is the Creator and Job, the created.[10] God reminded Job of a simple fact that we don't always so easily accept. It is God's world, and He can do with it whatever He wants. In fact, Job is a book more about God's sovereignty than it is about persevering under trial.

God Vindicates, But Is Not Vindictive

Furthermore and also vitally important to remember, God's anger at sin is not a malignant or malicious retaliation – inflicting injury for no reason or in return for an injury received. God vindicates, but He is not vindictive.[11] He takes no perverse pleasure in punishing sin, but neither does He punish with a heavy heart or a saddened demeanor.

Is Hell Fair?

Most often we think that our perception is reality. Most people look at God's punishment of sin as the grossest injustice ever seen in the universe. They find it to be the grandest example of unfairness and discrimination on a cosmic mind-numbing scale – so much so, that most dismiss the idea of a righteous and just God outright: "If God is this cruel to punish the innocent, then I want no part of Him."

Consider this perspective: accept for a moment that we are all guilty and living under a death sentence. The world around us should be more than enough evidence to convince you of this truth – that we are indeed fallen. Guilt – not innocence is our state. Our sentence is fixed in place; life only delays our inevitable and ultimate fate. Our physical death will usher all of us into our eternal separation from God.

Then came the cross, and the situation changed. Now salvation is available to those who believe in the sacrifice of Christ. "Justice confronts the changed position and pronounces the believing just."[12]

No one is cheated or treated unfairly. Before the cross all were lost; now because of the cross millions upon millions of people are saved. This is the perspective and way of the Holy One. This is the way we are to view God's working His grace in His creation.

Is Forgiveness Fair?

In *The Reason for God*, Timothy Keller recounts a conversation he once had with a woman who thought the idea of a judging God and the existence of hell was offensive. He asked her:

"'Why aren't you offended by the idea of a forgiving God?' She looked puzzled. I continued, 'I respectfully urge you to consider your cultural location when you find the Christian teaching about hell offensive.' I went on to point out that secular Westerners get upset by the Christian doctrine of hell, but they find Biblical teaching about turning the other cheek and forgiving enemies appealing. I then asked her to consider how someone from a different culture sees Christianity. In traditional societies the teaching about 'turning the other cheek' makes absolutely no sense. It offends people's deepest instincts about what is right."[13]

Why should our Western cultural worldview be the deciding factor in whether or not a God that judges is fair? Those opposed to the premise of hell are often those who are opposed to the very idea that people like Jeffrey Dahmer can be forgiven and allowed into heaven for their simple belief in the cross and the sacrifice of Christ. If hell offends you, a God who is willing to forgive should also be offensive to you.

Our Role and Responsibility

J.I. Packer also has something to add about our responsibility in the matter of our eternal standing.

"God's wrath in the Bible is something men choose for themselves. Before hell is an experience inflicted by God, it is a state for which man himself opts, by retreating from the light which God shines in his heart to lead him to Himself."[14]

The most well known verse in the Bible is John 3:16, but the verses that follow explain our role in rejecting the light and salvation of Christ. Start at John 3:16, but keep reading past the familiar:

"For God did not send His Son into the world to condemn the world, but to save the world through Him. Whoever believes in Him is not condemned, but whoever does not believe stands condemned already because he has not believed in the name of God's one and only Son. This is the verdict: Light has come into the world, but men loved darkness instead of light because their deeds were evil."
(John 3:17-19)

An Accurate Litmus Test?

This question of God's righteousness and justice is a pivotal one in how you see Him. Your view on His anger (His wrath directed toward sin) is a true and accurate test of your heart's attitude toward God. Your position on this one topic is a clear indication of whether or not the God you believe in is the one revealed to us in the Scriptures, or if

He is a God you are creating because He best fits the wishes of what you want Him to be.

We all must ask ourselves, "Is my God the God of the Bible or the God of my own wishful thinking?" This hope we have that God is too kind to punish those who reject Him is a dangerous and deadly way of thinking. It relieves our fear of judgment and gives us a freedom to live a lifestyle of our own choosing. Responsible and fully aware moral beings are not wise to take this gamble with their eternal future.[15]

Why "God is Righteous" is a BIG DEAL

Of all the Big Deal sections, this may be the most important. There are consequences that must be faced if we dismiss the fact that God is righteous and just.

We need to recognize our sin and repent. We must not merely acknowledge our sin but make an active effort to turn from it every day.

We need to have a healthy fear of God that motivates us toward living a holy lifestyle. Our lives are to be set apart, different, and not assimilated to the world around us.

Praise should come easily from a heart of sincere gratitude. We should realize all that we have been saved from – that our salvation is a free gift, unearned, and undeserved.

There are consequences, and God does repay evil. Not forgiving those who have done you wrong, is evidence of not believing that God is just. You may be tempted to take revenge and to get even when you are sinned against. But remember that God is righteous – and other's sins toward you will one day be addressed and accounted for, because in reality their sin was against God – not you.

Believers should be motivated to share their faith with others. We should all have a heartfelt burden for those without Christ. Our love for others should be larger than our fear of sharing His truth.

We need to recognize that God is protecting us from further evil. He is promoting the spiritual health of the world by being just and confronting sin in the measure that He does. If God were not righteous, evil would go unchecked, without restraint. If there were no moral code, chaos would reign, and the world would be a place of evil to a magnitude we can barely imagine.[16]

We cannot complain about how God acts. Because God loves justice and because we are created in His image, we are born with a desire for fairness. We want bad people punished and good people rewarded. But we have no reason to complain about how God does (or does not) pass out His judgment to others. Because justice once directed at us was poured out on Another, and since we are made clean by the action of Another, we have no right to dictate how God must act.[17]

We cannot argue with God about how He acts. This point was made in a sermon by Charles Spurgeon 120 years ago:

> "Do not fence with God or quarrel with Scripture, but as His Word declares that the wicked shall be cast into Hell with all the nations that forget God, admit that you deserve to be so dealt, for you deserve it."[18]

We have no footing to argue with God about how He administers His justice. In fact, it may be the height of all human arrogance to do so.

We cannot expect to understand how God acts. Chan wrote in *Erasing Hell* of how important it is for us to "let God be God."

> "This book is actually much more than a book on hell. It's a book about embracing a God who isn't always easy to understand, and whose ways are far beyond us; a God whose thoughts are much higher than our thoughts; a God who, as the sovereign Creator and Sustainer of all things, has every right to do as the psalmist says, 'whatever He pleases.' (Ps. 115:3 NASB) God has the right to do WHATEVER He pleases."[19]

In the end, your opinions are not the ones that matter. There is a mystery about God and how He works that you must accept, even if you find yourself unwilling or unable to embrace it.

Our feelings can never dictate what is true. Francis Chan goes on to explain that our feelings may or may not line up with our beliefs and our theology, and they don't have to.

> "As I have said all along, I don't *feel like* believing in hell. And yet I do. Maybe someday I will stand in complete agreement with Him, but for now I attribute the discrepancy to an underdeveloped sense of justice on my part. God is perfect. And I joyfully submit to a God whose ways are much, much higher than mine."[20]

The prophet Isaiah said pretty much the same thing 2,700 years ago:

> "For My thoughts are not your thoughts, neither are your ways
> My ways, as the heavens are higher than the earth, so are My ways
> higher than your ways and My thoughts than your thoughts."
> (Isaiah 55:8-9)

Reflection Questions:

1. Which Big Deal point speaks the loudest to you?
2. Take a moment to rank the Big Deal points from 1 to 10 in your order of importance.
3. What would the world look like without God's righteousness and moral code?
4. How do we see this attribute played out in the life of Christ?
5. What will it take for people to realize the seriousness of hell and punishment?
6. Why is it hard to let God have revenge when we are wronged?
7. Because God is righteous and just, I will . . .

"Think-On-It" Verse:

"Then Peter began to speak: 'I now realize how true it is that God does not show favoritism but accepts men from every nation who fear Him and do what is right.'"
Acts 10:34-35

"Where can I go from Your Spirit? Where can I flee from Your presence? If I go up to the heavens, You are there; if I make my bed in the depths, You are there. If I rise on the wings of the dawn, if I settle on the far side of the sea, even there Your hand will guide me, Your right hand will hold me fast."
Psalm 139:7-10

7 - God is All Present

Whiffle What? . . . in the Where?

They were playing whiffle-ball in the church sanctuary?! The youth group just had an all-night lock-in where they ate a lot of pizza, played some goofy games, slept very little, and enjoyed a game of whiffle-ball at 2:00 a.m. in the sanctuary. How do you feel about whiffle-ball, hide-and-seek or any game playing in the space where you worship on Sunday morning? Why do you feel that way?

You may have mixed feelings about whiffle-ball in the sanctuary. There are two sides of the argument. Those opposed will say, "This is God's house, a sacred space." Those who favor whiffle-ball rightly point out that God is everywhere, all of the time, and not just in the church sanctuary.

God is omnipresent which means God is "all present." Since God is infinite, His being knows no boundaries. So obviously He is everywhere. This truth is taught repeatedly throughout the Bible. The phrase "I am with you always" is repeated a total of 22 times in the Scriptures. These words were even spoken by Jesus before He ascended to heaven (Matthew 28:20).

There are doctrines found in the Scriptures that take some effort to fully understand; the omnipresence of God is not one of them. The passages supporting this truth are so plain and numerous that it would actually take some effort on our part to misunderstand and deny them.[1]

Forever Everywhere and All at Once

There is no place that you could go to escape God's presence. He is not limited by time or space. He is present at every point of time and space. This can only happen because God is also eternal, which means God has always been everywhere all at once. He is also everywhere in equal measure.

When we use the prefix "omni" – we are not only indicating that God is everywhere, but also how much of Him is everywhere. He is not only present everywhere; He is fully present everywhere. This theological term is known as His "immensity." Christians around the world enjoy and experience the fullness of His presence wherever they are. This immensity of God is not referring to His size, but to His ability to be fully present everywhere, all at once.[2]

God Does Not Live in Your Church
So what about whiffle-ball in the sanctuary? If God is infinite and everywhere, then He is everywhere in the exact same measure. There is not more of God in your church building. There is not less of God in a casino or a local biker bar or even a Las Vegas night club.

Now, chances are you are not going to *feel* much of God's presence in a Las Vegas nightclub, even though He is there. In turn, you may feel more of God's presence in a beautiful cathedral because of the atmosphere and the aesthetics of that place. You may even feel God's presence in a small and dingy storefront church, because you have memories of previously meeting with God in that place.

Your church building is not "God's house." But that doesn't mean whiffle-ball in the sanctuary is always a good idea either. Even though God is everywhere in equal measure, you probably will *feel* His presence in some places more than others. If people in your church see the sanctuary as a sacred space, it may be a good idea to skip the midnight whiffle-ball out of respect for them and their perspective on things.

Differently in Different Places
While God is everywhere in equal measure, He also reserves the right to act differently in different places. He is always present to bless us when we are alone in times of personal study and prayer. He also promises to bless us with His presence when we worship and pray together with others. But also at times God is present in a place not to bless, but to punish. This allows a holy God to be present everywhere, even in the depths of hell.[3]

Why "God is Everywhere" is a BIG DEAL
The Bad News: No one can hide from God. Jonah tried and learned firsthand that this is impossible. God is present with us in every situation. When you choose to sin, He is fully aware at that very

moment of the choices you are making. When we recognize this, it should help us make wiser choices.

The phrase "practical atheist" is often used to describe someone who believes in God yet lives his life as though God did not exist. Everyone must answer the question, "If God is here and real, does my life or my actions look any different than if He wasn't?"

The Good News: God cannot hide from us. Even when we are walking through the most difficult of circumstances, God is always there. We should find great comfort in knowing that we never walk through this life and its trials alone.

> "Even though I walk through the valley of the shadow
> of death, I will fear no evil, for You are with me."
> (Psalm 23:4)

24/7/365 Help: If God is everywhere, we should also realize that besides helping us to avoid sinful situations, God's presence is available to help us serve Him in every circumstance. You are never alone in whatever opportunity God provides for you to have an impact in the life of another. God is always there to help you serve others.

Worship: We experience God's presence more intently when we worship Him knowing that He is always present when we gather – regardless of where we are or how many are present. The Bible says the rocks themselves would cry out to worship God if no one else would (Luke 19:40).

No More Holy of Holies: In the Old Testament, God's Holy Spirit dwelled in the Holy of Holies found in the traveling tabernacle and then in the Temple of Jerusalem. When Christ died on the cross, the veil that separated the Holy of Holies was torn in two (Matthew 27:51).

This is a powerful illustration to show that the Holy Spirit no longer lives in one central place, but within all of us. When you put your faith in Christ alone and ask Him to forgive you of your sins, you then become a temple of the Holy Spirit, and He promises to live in you.

Reflection Questions:

1. How have you justified sinning, knowing that God is always present with you?
2. What would it mean if God were not omnipresent?
3. Describe a situation when you felt alone. How does this truth impact those thoughts and feelings?
4. How do you feel about whiffle-ball in the sanctuary? Why? Do you have a "sacred spot?"
5. How do you feel about God's being fully present in a casino or other "ungodly" places?
6. How can remembering this attribute help enhance your worship?
7. Because God is omnipresent, I will . . .

"Think-On-It" Verse:

"Do not let your hearts be troubled. Trust in God; trust also in Me. I will ask the Father, and He will give you another Counselor to be with you forever – the Spirit of truth. The world cannot accept Him, because it neither sees Him nor knows Him. But you know Him, for He lives with you and will be in you. I will not leave you as orphans; I will come to you."
John 14:1, 16-18

"Lord, You have made the heavens and the earth by Your great power and outstretched arm. Nothing is too hard for You."

Jeremiah 32:17

8 - God is All Powerful

Everything is Evenly Easy

One of my favorite Far Side cartoons is a drawing of God rolling out a piece of clay in His hands into a long, tube-like shape. The picture shows Him thinking to Himself, "Man, these things are a cinch." The caption below the picture says simply, "God makes a snake."

We easily fall into the habit of thinking that some things are harder for God to do than other things. Creating a snake is easy but creating an elephant or the planet Saturn with its rings is way more difficult. This is a faulty way of thinking about God and His power. Everything is evenly easy to Him.

"To the infinite, all finites are equal." If God is indeed infinite, then everything He does is evenly easy for Him.[1] There are no big or little miracles; there's just God doing His thing. In fact, every single action is done without effort. He spends no energy that needs to be refreshed or replenished. Because He is self-sufficient, He has no need to look anywhere else for power or strength. He never gets tired. All the power needed to do whatever He desires is found in His infinite being.[2]

Omnipotence means that God is all powerful – that He has unlimited power. This unlimited power allows Him to carry out His holy and sovereign will. Because God is omnipotent, nothing can stop His decreed will from happening; nothing can slow down or stop His plans from being fulfilled.

God is Almighty. The Bible tells us 56 times that God is Almighty – not "really, really strong" or "pretty amazing," but Almighty. That word is never used to describe anyone else. He alone is Almighty.[3] At this point it might be fair to ask whether your God is Almighty or just pretty amazing.

Does God Ever Need a Breather?

One day our daughter asked us if God ever gets tired. She asked because on Sunday she had sung, "The King is exhausted, forever exhausted on high, I will praise Him!" There is a big difference between our King being exalted and exhausted. Fortunately, "the King is exalted, forever exalted!"

God creates and sustains all things, yet He never grows weary or tired (Isaiah 40:27-31). When the Bible says God rested on the seventh day, it was to set an example for us and our need for rest, not because He was tired and needed rest. God doesn't need to relax, unwind, or rest up for the busy week ahead of planet spinning, asteroid supervision, and global tide control. God is forever exalted, but never exhausted.

Omnipotence and His Other Attributes
God's attributes are tied together in some pretty amazing ways as they work together to accomplish His will. This is true for His omnipotence as well. God's sovereignty and omnipotence must go together in order for God to reign and be sovereign over His creation. He must have all power.[4]

But God's omnipotence must also be accompanied by His unending attribute of wisdom. God is wise, and He knows what is best for this world and for us as individuals. So He must also have infinite power in order to execute His will and what He deems good and wise.[5]

Omnipotence and Our Freedom
It only stands to reason, that since God is infinite and since He possesses power, then He must possess infinite power. But it is also true that He allows His creatures to have some limited power. This delegation of power that is given to us in no way diminishes His own sovereignty. God allows us freedom to exercise our limited free will; still He is ultimately the one in charge.

God Cannot Do Everything
God is infinite, all powerful, without limits. Yet there are some things God cannot do. He cannot do anything that is inconsistent with His nature, character, and purpose. He cannot do anything that is contrary to His character. For example, God is incapable of lying.[6] So when we talk of God's omnipotence, we must always think of it in the context of Him doing His holy will and not Him doing absolutely everything that we can imagine Him being able to do. He can do everything only to the extent that it is consistent with His character.

The "Laws of Nature" and Cheating the Creator
Science has accomplished many amazing things. Technology has given us the ability to do things that past generations could not even have dreamed of. Advances in the medical field allow us to transplant

organs and ward off diseases that used to kill and maim. We see stars no one ever dreamed of seeing. We've walked on the moon, and we've seen inside a single cell. It's all pretty amazing stuff.

But there is a downside to the progress of science. The more "intelligent" we become, the greater the difference between the modern mindset and the mindset of past generations. Where once we saw God, now we see only the "laws of nature." In the past, God ruled the world; but in modern thinking, the world rules itself.[7] We are seemingly here only to be caretakers of it in some measure.

The word *law* really has two meanings. First, it can be used to describe the external rule enforced by authority (such as the laws against stealing and murder). Secondly, it can be used to explain the way things run in the universe. For example, the law of gravity.

Here we can call into question this second use of the word. What we observe about our world and universe is the way God works and sustains His creation. In truth, it is His power at work – not laws in the technical sense per se.[8] We call them laws of nature, in part, because then accountability to God is removed.

Why is this important? Because our God is not getting the credit that is due Him for the power He shows every day in His creation. God's omnipotence is responsible for everything you see every day, and "Mother Nature" is usurping what rightfully belongs to Him.

Science and the Supernatural
The omnipotent God is actively sustaining His creation moment by moment – holding, guiding, directing, and controlling all that He has made (Hebrews 1:3, Colossians 1:17). It can even be argued that there is no "law" of gravity, but only the great probability that God will act in such a consistent way that objects will continually fall as if there were a "law" of gravity.

When God chooses to suspend these probabilities, these "supernatural" occurrences are then called miracles. If this is true, then miracles aren't all that supernatural; they are simply special events purposed by God. A miracle is an exception to God's probability. God chooses to act in ways of extremely high probability in order to maintain order. The fact that moment by moment God sustains His creation through His omnipotent power demonstrates His infinite power.

But this sustaining omnipotence also shows us that God is good, caring, concerned, and personable. Regardless of what is happening on this planet, there is a loving, omnipotent being who is in charge. Our lives are not left to mere chance or chaos. There is great stability, security, and comfort to be found when our God is omnipotent.

Why "God is All Powerful" is a BIG DEAL

There is great peace and reassurance to be found. The same power God used to create the universe is also at hand to assure our salvation. He has shown this great power throughout the scriptures. It was seen at the parting of the Red Sea, the fire being called down on Mount Carmel, and the resurrection of Christ. Nothing can frustrate His plans for the future.

There are no "maverick molecules" that are loose and not under His control. We see the forces in this world that threaten and cause worry, but in truth, we can live without fear and rest in the fact that nothing can withstand His power.[9]

We can pray with boldness for God to do whatever He wants. We think too small. As a result, our prayers are also too small. Instead of praying reactively for our problems to just go away, we should pray proactively for God to do amazing things. Our prayers should be earth-shaking requests that will glorify God by asking Him to do great things.

Prayer is the simple admission that God is rich, and we are poor. The bigger our requests, the more honor we show God. You can insult the richest person on the planet by asking him for only one dollar; you pay him a greater respect when you boldly ask him for something bigger.

Realize your weakness actually allows God's power to be seen in you. We assume that when we are strong and feeling confident, God's power will be seen is us, but the exact opposite is true.

> "But He said to me, 'My grace is sufficient for you, for My power is made perfect in weakness.' Therefore I will boast all the more gladly about my weaknesses, so that Christ's power may rest on me."
> (2 Corinthians 12:9)

Remember, God is in charge – not Satan. Don't give Satan more credit than he is due. Satan is only allowed to act as God permits. The battle between God and Satan is not a boxing match where they trade blows and inflict pain upon each other. When God decides, Satan will be defeated forever with a wisp of God's breath.

When trouble hits, prayer should be our first response – like the reflex action that happens when a doctor hits your knee with that little rubber hammer. This will only happen when you recognize the power of God. The word *impossible* can never be used in reference to God.

We should be more willing to obey and less reluctant to serve. When we see our God as truly Almighty, then we can trust Him to help us accomplish great things such as living more obediently and serving Him more effectively, with greater vision and love for others.

Reflection Questions:

1. How have you seen the power of God at work in your own life?
2. Describe a situation where you failed to trust in the power of God.
3. Where do we see examples of Christ possessing this attribute?
4. What would it say about God if He were not omnipotent?
5. Why do we doubt His omnipotence?
6. Why do we so often believe in the big miracles of the Bible, but still wrestle with doubt?
7. Because God is omnipotent, I will . . .

"Think-On-It" Verse:
"With man this is impossible, but
with God all things are possible."
Matthew 19:26

"Lord, You have searched me and You know me.
You know when I sit and when I rise; You perceive
my thoughts from afar. You discern my going out
and my lying down; You are familiar with all my ways.
Before a word is on my tongue You know it completely."
Psalm 139:1-4

9 - God is All Knowing

Our Returning Champion ... Again
Ken Jennings is noted for holding the record for the longest winning
streak on the TV game show, *Jeopardy!* In 2004, Jennings won 74
straight games before he was defeated on his 75th appearance. His total
earnings on *Jeopardy!* were $3,022,700. No offense to Mr. Jennings, but
God would kill him in a game of *Jeopardy!* God would be able to
answer the questions before they were ever uttered aloud. He knows
everything. We call this omniscience.

As kids, my sister and I knew there was "someone" watching over us,
paying close attention to all we did. We knew we had to live our lives
in a way to make him happy because we heard that he knew everything
about us. He would reward us if we were good and punish us if we
were bad. Unfortunately, this "someone" was not God – it was Santa
Claus. God alone, not Santa, knows everything about you.

The infinite knowledge of God has been described this way:
"He knows everything; everything possible, everything actual; all
events and all creatures of the past, present and of the future. He
is perfectly acquainted with every detail in the life of every being in
heaven, in earth, and in hell (Daniel 2:22). Nothing escapes His
notice, nothing can be hidden from Him, nothing is forgotten by
Him."[1]

Yet *Another* Thing God Cannot Do?
As mentioned earlier, God cannot sin or do anything else contrary to
His character. But there is also another thing God cannot do – He
cannot learn. God possesses perfect knowledge, which means He has
no need to learn.

In fact, God has never learned anything because He simply can't. If
omniscience means "all-knowing" then God knows everything already,
and His knowledge is infinite. In fact, at the very moment God did
learn something, He would cease to be God as we know Him.[2]

There are No Surprises to God

Omniscience means "all knowing." God has unlimited knowledge. This infinite knowledge is what qualifies Him as Sovereign Ruler and Righteous Judge over everything. Since He knows everything, we can trust that His justice will always be administered fairly.

Not only does God know everything that will happen; He also knows everything that can *possibly* happen. You can never surprise Him. He never wonders about anything. Since God is omniscient, He knows what we are thinking at any given moment. It is impossible to hide anything from Him. He knows our motives and our hearts' desires (Job 37:16; Psalm 147:5). He does not seek information from us to complete His knowledge or understanding. In the Scriptures, when God asked questions, it was only to engage people in conversation so He could impart the truth He desires to communicate to us.[3]

God is the Ultimate Multitasker

Some of us are pretty good multitaskers; we have the ability to do a number of things all at once. We can simultaneously drive a car, eat a hamburger, adjust the radio, and talk on the cell phone – and most of the time, do so without having a traffic accident.

God alone has the ability to hear a billion people praying all at once. We have no reason to worry that our requests will not be heard. There is no danger that we as individuals will be overlooked amidst the millions and millions of people who present their needs to an infinite God. He is able to give equal attention to everyone all at once, as if He were listening to only one person at a time.[4]

The Big Question

A question we often ask is how God's omniscience co-exists with our free will to make decisions. If God really knows every decision that we are going to make, are we really free? Some argue that God does not know the things that cannot yet be known because the actions and decisions of free people are not yet made.

The obvious problem with this position is that it denies God any knowledge of the future. This is inconsistent with the many passages of Scripture where we are told of God's knowledge of future events. It also conflicts with dozens of prophetic passages found in the Old Testament where God predicted the future in great detail.[5]

Ultimately, the belief that God does not know our future decisions falls short because it attempts to explain the unexplainable – the relationship between God's omniscience and our free will. He must be understood through faith, for "without faith it is impossible to please Him" (Hebrews 11:6). As long as we endeavor to understand the infinite with our finite minds, we will always fall short of fully comprehending how God's sovereignty and our free will co-exist.

Why "God is All Knowing" is a BIG DEAL

A Comfort: Some find great comfort, security, and reassurance in knowing that God is always aware of their paths and their activities. To them this is a good thing, a blessing. It's to their delight that He understands how they feel and even what they think.

God knows and always knew all the awful things we've done (and will do in the future). In spite of this, He loves us and calls us into His family. Chris Tiegreen writes:

> "Once we realize that He sees us as we truly are, and understand that He has offered us this wonderful invitation to be saved and loved by Him anyway, we can relax in utter security. He has seen our worst and it has not sent Him running in the other direction."[6]

A Curse: To others, the idea of God's omniscience is a curse. It is an attribute of God that many wish they had the power to strip from Him.[7] For many, it's unsettling to know that their actions and their paths are watched by the Almighty God. They don't see God as loving; they see Him as a "cosmic watchdog" or as an "oppressive chaperone" only here to clamp down on their fun. They would rather hide their activities from God because they know they are sinful.

A Consideration: What about you? How you view this attribute and the fact that you cannot hide anything from God is another test of how you see Him. (Do you want Him to know everything? Or is it unsettling to you that He does?) No one can lie to God or deceive Him in any way. He knows everything about us and why we do what we do. Knowing this should be helpful in keeping us accountable and desiring to live a life that's pleasing to Him.

Reflection Questions:

1. Do you think Jesus was omniscient while on earth? Explain your answer using Scripture.
2. What are the consequences if God is not omniscient?
3. God knows your motives. Does that encourage you or discourage you? What can you do about it?
4. Do you see God's omniscience as a comfort or a curse? Why?
5. Why is it hard to comprehend God's omniscience?
6. How can we find security in God's omniscience?
7. Because God is omniscient, I will . . .

"Think-On-It" Verse:

"You have set our iniquities before You, our secret sins in the light of Your presence."
Psalm 90:8

"For this is what the high and lofty One says: He who lives forever, whose name is holy: I live in a high and holy place."
Isaiah 57:15

10 - God is Transcendent

Rotary Phones and Eight Track Tapes

One day in the car my daughter kept playing with the window in the back seat. When I told her to stop rolling the window up and down, she asked, "What does *roll* mean?"

I then realized she had never "rolled down" a window in her entire life. Even though our cars were never anything special (trust me on this), car windows in her world had always gone up or down with the push of a button and not the turning of a handle.

Today we don't use words that were quite common in years past. Words like bloomers, fortnight, courting, codger, and sawbuck are words from the past that are hardly used today. My grandma always used the word *icebox* when talking about her refrigerator. When she was growing up, it was a box kept cold with a huge chunk of ice. As times change, so does our vocabulary.

Having a Fear and Awe of God

Think about the phrase "God-fearing." When was the last time you heard someone described as a "God-fearing" man or a "God-fearing" woman? Today we use phrases like "He really loves the Lord" or "She's a really committed believer." Our phraseology has changed, largely because our mindset has also changed. We no longer fear God or respect those who do.

Even if we use the words *awe* or *respect* in place of the word *fear*, we still have largely lost that sense of awe and majesty that is due the Almighty God of the universe. In the past, people of faith spoke of fearing and revering God no matter how intimate their communion was with Him.

At the very foundation of religious life was this idea that God was awesome, and our actions could, in reality, be very damaging to us. In the past, there was more of a sense that God was very different from us. A belief that God is transcendent is seen throughout the Scriptures. It was part of the DNA of biblical characters. This fear of God was more than an apprehension or danger; it was an acute feeling of insufficiency in the presence of God.[1]

When we aren't in awe of God, we don't see Him as transcendent. When we don't understand what His transcendence means, we won't have the proper awe of Him.

Is God "Weird" to You?

Weird is a negative word. No one likes to be described as weird. But the truth is, God is weird. He is unlike anything or anyone else. He is far beyond our most inspired conceptions of Him. God is transcendent. He is exceedingly far above and beyond creation. He is both greater than creation and independent of it. If *weird* means "different" – then God should be weird to you because He is totally different than we are and totally different from what we normally understand Him to be.

We don't do well with the idea of transcendence and not being able to fully comprehend God; as a result, we shrink Him down to something we can understand. At that very moment, God is not transcendent; He is then not above and beyond His creation. He is then not where He should be or needs to be.

God is not at the top of creation, with everything else in a descending order below Him. God is separate from His creation. There is a finite difference between an archangel and a caterpillar. But an infinite difference between that same archangel and God. Angels and caterpillars are both created, but the Creator of both stands apart. He is transcendent over His creation. He is not a part *of* it; He is apart *from* it. All created things fall into the category of "that which is not God" and are thereby infinitely separated from and different from Him.[2] Because of this, the intensity and depth of God's holiness, power, and majesty will always be beyond our ability to fully understand.

What is the "Kabōd" of God?

Brennan Manning explains the meaning of the Hebrew word *kabōd*. Over time it has actually had three meanings. First, it meant "the weight of an object, its heaviness" – something that could be weighed on a scale. Secondly, it came to mean "material wealth" or to describe someone who had achieved "rank, status, prominence and power." Finally, the Jewish community identified *kabōd* with the "weight, greatness, eminence, power, and authority of God" – the awesome majesty of God."[3]

As some words die because they become antiquated, some words evolve in order to express something deeper. *Kabōd* evolved from a weight, to a description of power and status, to a word that tries to

72

convey the power and majesty of God. God is the greatest of the great weights. His very presence is "heavy."

Manning goes on to explain what happens when we truly realize the kabōd or "otherness" of God:

"Kabōd is not a safe topic. It induces a feeling of terror before the Infinite and exposes as sham our empty religious talk, pointless activity, our idle curiosity and ludicrous pretensions of importance, our frantic busyness. The awareness that the eternal transcendent God of Jesus Christ is our absolute future gives us the shakes."[4]

As mentioned earlier, we desire a God that is present and close by to help us when we find ourselves in trouble. We gravitate to the Abba Father because that God gives us security and peace. When your God is *only* your Abba or "daddy" God, He is not the transcendent Kabōd.

The "Otherness" of God

If you've grown up in the church, have you ever heard a sermon series on the "otherness" of God? Have you ever even heard this idea that God is transcendent and dwells in inaccessible light? (1 Timothy 6:16) Do you really understand what happened at the transfiguration of Christ? I don't.

The Bible reports in Matthew 17:1-8 that while praying, Christ's appearance changed. His face shone like the sun, His clothing became dazzling white, and He had a conversation with Moses and Elijah about His coming death. How many sermons have you heard about this amazing, pivotal, and confusing event?

Manning goes on to explain our hesitancy to dwell on the transcendence of God. He writes:

"Small wonder there is a deafening silence from our pulpits and publishers about the transcendent character of God Almighty. And who can blame us? Throughout the history of salvation God has revealed His presence but never His essence. Since the Holy One is unknowable, we can only stutter and stammer about the omnipotent deity who, with effortless ease, created a star 264 trillion miles away...."[5]

There is something much different than we know – there is something transcendent about this God of ours. He's more than just *above;* He also exists *apart* from His creation.

"Hide or Die" and the Baby Jesus

When Moses asked to see God's glory, he was denied. He was told to hide his face or else he would die from the experience of this divine encounter. God protected Moses in a cleft of a rock and allowed him a glimpse only after He passed by (Exodus 33:18-23). This is as accurate a picture of God as is Jesus lying in the manger as a baby. Our view of God must have balance; He is both a blinding light and a loving Savior who cares for us as His children.

This contrast is vividly seen in the opening chapters of Genesis. A transcendent God spoke all of creation and humanity into existence. Shortly afterward we see that He experienced an intimate fellowship with those created in His image – an intimacy that would be destroyed by the introduction of sin.

Why "God is Transcendent" is a BIG DEAL

Continual reminder: God's ways are higher than ours. Our hopes and plans are simply that – hopes and plans. God has infinite wisdom to run His universe. His transcendence allows us a deep faith in Him and His plans for us.

The cross matters: God reveals Himself to us and allows us to have lasting fellowship with Him. Our sins are atoned for through the death and resurrection of Christ. Again, having a proper balance is the key. God is infinite and transcendent, but also personal and intimate.

Worship: Transcendence and majesty are "a declaration of His greatness and an invitation to worship."[6] God is not far from us in distance, but far above us in greatness. That alone is reason enough to praise, worship, and adore Him. Worship of God is our simple acknowledgment that there is one who is far more worthy of our allegiance than ourselves.

It reminds us of our proper position: We are not equal partners with God in some sort of contractual partnership. We make the assumption, "If I do this for God, then He will do this for me." This is not the case.

It's good for us: Recognizing the transcendent nature of God is beneficial to us. There is a price to be paid for avoiding His transcendence and unknowability. The loss of embracing this "otherness" of God has caused great harm to Christian spirituality in the life of the individual believer. The casualties include our silent reverence, our radical amazement, and an affectionate awe at the infinite goodness of God. These three traits are defined in the expression, "fearing the Lord."[7]

This silent reverence, radical amazement, and affectionate awe are essential parts of this relationship. But when God is *only* your Abba Father, when He is only your "buddy," He is not the transcendent Kabōd.

Reflection Questions:

1. Describe the transfiguration event (Matthew 17:1-8) in your own words. What happened and why?
2. Do you fear God? How is fearing God different from respecting or highly esteeming Him?
3. Why do you worship God? What is your motivation most of the time?
4. How is your worship of God affected when you see Him as transcendent?
5. In the past, have you seen God as *apart from* creation or *at the top of* creation? Explain.
6. Why are we uncomfortable talking about the "otherness" of God?
7. Because God is transcendent, I will . . .

"Think-On-It" Verse:

"He sits enthroned above the circle of the earth, and its people are like grasshoppers. He stretches out the heavens like a canopy, and spreads them out like a tent to live in."
Isaiah 40:22

"I the Lord do not change."
Malachi 3:6

11 - God is Unchanging

Why is there a Drum Set in Our Whiffle-Ball Area?!
When it comes to change, people are funny, and when I say funny, I mean odd and perplexing. As a young man, my grandfather helped convince the leaders of his church to have their worship service in English instead of Swedish. He saw the need for change because, as crazy as it might sound, not everyone was speaking Swedish on the north side of Chicago in the 1940's. Change was needed.

Now flash forward fifty years to the day they moved a drum set into the sanctuary at his church. That was a change that he could do without. My grandfather went from a force for change to a stumbling block against it. What changed? He did. His perspective, his vision, and even his priorities had changed.

Change happens every day. Our kids grow up before our very eyes, technology continually opens new doors and opportunities, even our maps change as counties that used to be divided unite or vice versa. Change is inevitable and unavoidable.

The Church has also changed, and we're not just talking about drum sets in sanctuaries. Some change has certainly been for the better; some, for the worse. Where certain practices and behaviors were once seen as sinful, they are now seen as acceptable in far too many congregations and places of worship.

The Bible is very clear on this topic: God does not change. And that is a good thing. In a world that is constantly changing, God is the constant rock we can always depend on.

God's Public Relations "Problem"
Many people wish God would change. If He ever hired a public relations agent, I'm sure he would be advising God on the changes necessary to make Him more popular and acceptable to the general public.

For instance, the claim of Jesus as the *only* way to the Father (John 14:6) shows little or no tolerance in the eyes of many. This desire to see God change has fueled the misconceptions that a lot of people have about Him. If you don't like the way God is, you can simply imagine Him to be the way you want Him to be.

Fortunately God doesn't change to accommodate our wishes. His unchangeableness is defined this way:
> "God is unchanging in His being, perfections, purposes and promises, yet God does act and feel emotions, and He acts and feels differently in response to different situations."[1]

Another Thing God Cannot Do

The truth is, God simply cannot change even if He wanted to; His perfection does not allow for it. He cannot change for the better or be improved in any way. He can never be more holy than He is now. He can never be less holy in the future.[2] Technically; by definition, perfection cannot change.

Arthur Pink had this to say about God and His unchangeableness:
> "Immutability is one of the Divine perfections which is not sufficiently pondered. It is one of the excellencies of the Creator which distinguishes Him from all His creatures. God is perpetually the same: subject to no change in His being, attributes, or determinations. Therefore God is compared to a rock (Deuteronomy 32:4) which remains unmovable ..."[3]

What if God Could Change?

What scares you? Spiders? Snakes? Heights? Flying? Dark places? We all have different fears that we must face from time to time, but the scariest thing that I can think of is a God who can change. That is a very scary thought – a spine-chilling thought, to be honest with you.

Consider for a moment the implications of a God who could change. If God could change, then any change would have to be for either the better or the worse. If God changed for the better, then was He really sufficient when we trusted Him? How can we be sure that He is sufficient and fully capable for us now? Or, if it's possible for God to change for the worse, then what kind of God might He be in the future?[4] There is no sure foundation for anything if God could change.

While it is true that God does not change, He is also a God who keeps things from getting boring. God is not unrealistic, He is not inconsistent, but He is unpredictable. He rarely works as we think He should.

Our Change is Both Necessary and Beneficial

We have no choice but to experience change even if we don't want to; it's not an option for us. The law of mutation belongs to the fallen world. This change, this mutation, works against us in that it ultimately leads to our death. But in God, believers find a lasting and eternal permanence.[5]

Our lives are in a constant state of change. For those who do not believe in God, change is temporary, superficial, and ultimately without true meaning. But for those who follow Christ, changes are purposed for a reason – to conform us into the image of Christ. Change is not only unavoidable; it's necessary and essential in our lives.

> "And we, who with unveiled faces all reflect the Lord's glory, are being transformed into His likeness with ever-increasing glory."
> (2 Corinthians 3:18)

God is Our Rock

God is the permanence in our lives upon which we can always depend. "Human nature cannot be relied upon; but God can! However unstable I may be, however fickle my friends may prove, God changes not."[6] We all long for the comfort and security of a God who cares. But what if that God who cares was also a God who changes? Our security in Him would always remain in doubt.

God is a Rock upon which we can always depend. Our emotions, moods, attitudes, and desires are always seemingly dependent upon our circumstances and our situations. Thankfully, God is not like that. His mood never changes toward us. He never cools off in His feelings for us.[7] His attitude toward us and our sin was the same in the Garden moments after the serpent's deception as it was when Christ cried out:

> "Come to me, all you who are weary and burdened, and I will give you rest."
> (Matthew 11:28)

Why would we even want a God who is willing and able to change? The truth is, we wish God would change, adapt, grow, and become a bit more flexible so He could better meet our desires. This is, in reality, an incredible display of arrogance. Do we really want the Almighty God to change for our own temporal wants and passing desires?

His Truth Does Not Change

If our God does not change, then it is also important to recognize that His truth also does not change. This is attested to in the Scriptures:

"The grass withers and the flowers fall,
but the word of our God stands forever"
(Isaiah 40:8)

"Your word, O Lord, is eternal; it stands firm in
the heavens. Long ago I learned from Your statutes
that You established them to last forever."
(Psalm 119:89,152)

We may want to be selective in which rules apply for us today and which ones don't, but God's truth does not change simply because we want it to. We need to always remember that the promises, purposes, and words of warning found in the Bible apply to us as well as to their first readers. They are not just historical; they are instructional and the "eternally valid revelation of the mind of God"[8] for all people, at all times – past, present, and future.

As believers, we need to re-evaluate from time to time our attitude toward the Scriptures. Do we really believe them to be the unchanging truth? The world has largely dismissed the Word of God as a relic, or as at least an outdated teaching that no longer applies to us and our world today. How do you see your Bible? Do you see it as His unchanging truth or merely a book of instruction, hope, and encouragement?

Why "God is Unchanging" is a BIG DEAL

Stability in this life is found only in the unchanging truth of God's Word. The teachings of the Scriptures can be fully trusted only when we realize that the God who made them does not change. His truth is the same now and forever.

Jesus told a parable in Matthew 7:24-27 of two builders. One built his house on the rock of Christ's teaching, the truth of God's Word. The other ignored the words of Christ and built his house on the shifting sand. When the storms came, the one house stood; the other fell with a great crash. We are to be a people who build our lives upon the unchanging truth of God and His Word.

Our hope is based on the unchanging promises of God. If God does not change, then His promises to us are also unchanging. The truths to which we cling in times of trial and struggle are firmly established for all eternity.

We are also able to trust God because our faith is rooted in an unchangeable supreme being. If God could change, our salvation would always be in doubt. The whole basis of our faith would fall apart.

If God does not change, the challenge then is for us to change. When difficulties come, we often blame God. We accuse Him of not being true to us and not living up to His end of the deal. We argue that we've been faithful to Him, but He has not been faithful to us in return.

When this happens, we often pray that God will change our circumstances and relieve us from our trial. But during times like these, it's actually most helpful to look at our own lives and consider where we may need to make changes in ourselves. We are the ones who must change. God loves us too much to let us stay the same.

Reflection Questions:

1. What would you like to change about God? Why?
2. Can we have the same close fellowship with Him as those in the Bible did? Explain.
3. Can we have the same power and strength when facing adversity as those in the Bible did? Explain.
4. Does God change His mind? (see the "Extra Stuff" Appendix)
5. What would happen if God did change? How would you feel about a God that changes?
6. What challenges have brought beneficial change to your life?
7. Because God does not change, I will . . .

"Think-On-It" Verse:

"God is not a man, that He should lie, nor a son of man, that He should change His mind. Does He speak and then not act? Does He promise and not fulfill?"
Numbers 23:19

> "All the peoples of the earth are regarded as nothing.
> He does as He pleases with the powers of heaven
> and the peoples of the earth. No one can hold back
> His hand or say to Him: 'What have you done?'"
> Daniel 4:35

12 - God is Sovereign

Life-Changing, Pivotal Moments

I think everyone has at least one pivotal moment in their life when they stare up into the sky and scream out of frustration, fear, or anxiety, "What the '#$@%' is going on?! Why is this happening to me?!" or "Is there anyone in charge up there?!"

We never have these thoughts when life is good. When you're at Disney World on a sunny day, God is good and His sovereignty is not in doubt. We only wrestle with these questions when things go wrong or it rains all week on your Florida vacation.

After a few disappointing or painful experiences are strung together, many conclude that no one is in charge. At that moment, they decide God is not sovereign. This is a natural conclusion for many when people experience the sudden death of a loved one, the torment of child abuse, or the shocking intensity of a life-changing accident or incident.

It's necessary to enter into this conversation on the sovereignty of God by fully acknowledging that the hurtful and painful experiences of the past are still a part the present-day equation in the lives of many. This is not an academic discussion for those who wrestle to accept this attribute of God.

To start, we need to define our terms. When we say God is sovereign, we are saying:

> "God is in control. He does whatever pleases Him and determines whether we can do what we have planned. This is the essence of God's sovereignty: His absolute independence to do as He pleases and His absolute control over the actions of His creatures. No creature, person, or empire can either thwart His will or act outside the bounds of His will.[1]

There are four keys words to consider when talking about the sovereignty of God: *Reconcile, Resolve, Recognize* and *Realize*.

81

RECONCILE: The Bible makes it quite clear that God is sovereign. You may need to reconcile this fact with experiences that may have left you feeling otherwise. Throughout the Scriptures, God is shown as being in charge. Pink defined it this way:

> "Being infinitely elevated above the highest creature, He is the Most High, Lord of heaven and earth. Subject to none, influenced by none, absolutely independent; God does as He pleases, only as He pleases, always as He pleases. None can thwart Him, none can hinder Him."[2]

> "My purpose will stand, and I will do all that I please."
> (Isaiah 46:10)

"Divine sovereignty means that God is God in fact as well as in name, that He is on the Throne of the universe, directing all things, working all things."[3] God is the one who "works out everything in conformity with the purpose of His will" (Ephesians 1:11).

An All-or-Nothing Proposition

We all have a choice to make: is God sovereign or not? Are you going to believe the Word of God or base your decisions on your own experiences? Are you going to accept only the good in life, and none of the bad? Will you allow the existence of evil to dictate whether or not you believe God is sovereign?

If the Bible is not true, if God is not in charge, then He is not omnipotent, not omniscient, and not omnipresent. If God is not sovereign, then He is not God. You really have no choice in the matter. If you believe in God, you must believe in a sovereign God. If the God you believe in is not in charge and not in control of everything, then He is not the God of the Scriptures. At that point He becomes *a* god, not *the* Almighty God.

It's not a matter of believing in God's sovereignty as much as *accepting* it. We have difficulty believing this because we have a hard time accepting the turns and circumstances that life can present. Our energies are best spent *accepting* God's sovereignty as opposed to trying to understand it.

Accepting God's sovereignty is not the same as merely submitting to it or resigning ourselves to it. Submission and resignation still have strong connotations of reluctance and fatalism. In effect you are saying, "God is sovereign; He can do what He likes, but I'm still not happy about it!" An attitude of accepting God's sovereign will also means that we are willing to trust His love for us and that He knows what's best for us. Admittedly, this is not easy in the midst of great pain and confusion.

RESOLVE: You need to resolve yourself to the fact that you have to accept some mysteries in life. The finite cannot fully comprehend the infinite. Ultimately, this challenge to resolve our need to understand the things of God is addressed by the following two passages:

> "The secret things belong to the Lord our God, but the
> things revealed belong to us and to our children forever,
> that we may follow all the words of this law."
> (Deuteronomy 29:29)

> "Now we see but a poor reflection as in a mirror;
> then we shall see face to face. Now I know in part;
> then I shall know fully, even as I am fully known."
> (1 Corinthians 13:12)

Much like trying to fully understand God's infinite nature, there are secret things that we will never fully know. God has not answered all the questions we have about sin, evil, misery, and our freedom to make choices. We need to let go of the desire to understand mysteries that will remain unsolved for now.

RECOGNIZE: We need to recognize the fact that God allows evil to exist for a reason. We need to recognize that our sovereign God uses everything (even evil) to bring glory to Himself.

> "He is the image of the invisible God, the firstborn over all
> creation. For by Him all things were created: things in heaven and
> on earth, visible and invisible, whether thrones or powers or rulers
> or authorities; all things were created by Him and for Him."
> (Colossians 1:15-16)

Using this text, John Piper makes it clear in his book, *Spectacular Sins,* that God uses everything to bring glory to His Son:

> "All that came into being exists for Christ - that is, everything
> exists to display the greatness of Christ. Nothing - nothing! - in the
> universe exists for its own sake. Everything - from the bottom of
> the oceans to the top of the mountains, from the smallest particles
> to the biggest star, from the most boring school subject to the
> most fascinating science, from the greatest saint to the most
> wicked genocidal dictator - everything that exists, exists to make
> the greatness of Christ more fully known - including you and the
> person you have the hardest time liking."[4]

As mind-blowing as it may seem, God uses everything, even the evil we witness each day, to bring glory to Himself. Sinful acts (even those seen on a grand scale) never nullify the decisive, Christ-exalting purposes of God. These "spectacular sins" do not just fail to nullify God's purposes; they are used by Him providentially to accomplish His will. Because of God's unfathomable and incomprehensible sovereignty, God is always able to make His Christ-exalting purposes come to pass.[5]

This truth is lived out in the example of Joseph and the interchange he had with his brothers. His proclamation that, "You meant it for evil, but God meant it for good" (Genesis 50:20) shows a providence of God in our lives that we can barely imagine, much less ever fully comprehend.

REALIZE: This may be the key word in our discussion of God's sovereignty. We need to realize how God works in His world and that His plans will always supersede our wants and needs.

When it comes to the topic of God's sovereignty, we usually start off by asking the wrong question. And asking the wrong question will always lead to the wrong conclusion. When we start the conversation by asking how the events of this world fit in with *our* rights and *our* needs, we are asking the wrong question. The question we must ask is this: How do the events of this world fit in with God's rights and His purposes for His planet?

Piper explains that our thinking about the sovereignty of God comes from either one of two places: a God-centered mindset or a man-centered mindset. Both are very different, with radically different starting points and conclusions.[6]

The Man-Centered Mindset
The man-centered mindset is not necessarily one that rules out God or even denies in principle that the Bible is true; however, it's a mindset that begins with man as the basic given reality in the universe. All of its thinking starts with the assumption that man has basic rights, basic needs, basic expectations. Then, moving out from this center, the man-centered mindset interprets the world with man and his rights and needs as the measure of all things.

What the man-centered mindset considers to be problems are deemed so because of how things fit or don't fit with its center – man and his rights, needs, and expectations. What this mindset considers to be

84

successes are deemed so because they fit with man and his rights, needs, and expectations.

This is the mindset with which we are born and one our society reinforces virtually every hour of every day of our lives. Paul called this mindset, "the mind that is set upon the flesh" (Romans 8:6-7), and said it is the way the natural person thinks (1 Corinthians 2:14). It is so much a part of us that we hardly know it's there. We just take it for granted until it collides with another mindset – the one in the Bible.

The God-Centered Mindset

The God-centered mindset (or Biblical mindset) is not simply one that includes God somewhere in the universe and says that the Bible is true. The God-centered mindset begins with a radically different starting point: God. It starts with God as the basic given reality in the universe. He was there before we or anything else were ever in existence. He is the only absolute reality.

The God-centered mindset starts with the assumption that God is the center of all reality. All thinking starts with the assumption that *God* has basic rights as the Creator of all things. He has goals that fit with His nature and perfect character. This mindset moves out from this center and interprets the world with God and *His* rights and goals as the measure of all things.

What the God-centered mindset sees as problems are usually not the same things the man-centered mindset sees as problems. The reason for this is because what makes something a problem in the God-centered mindset is not that it doesn't fit the rights and needs of man, but that it doesn't fit the rights and goals of God. If you start with man and his rights and wants, rather than starting with the Creator and His rights and goals, the problems of the universe will be very different.

The Basic Riddle of the Universe

Is the basic riddle of the universe how to preserve man's rights and solve his problems? Or is it how an infinitely worthy God can display the full range of His perfections – what Paul calls the "riches of His glory" (Romans 9:23) – His holiness, His power, His wisdom, His justice, His wrath, His goodness, His truth, and His grace?[7]

Turning the Tables

When I was a kid, my dad had a pastor friend whose wife left him for another man. I didn't know the whole story then; I still don't. But I do remember overhearing one conversation he had with my father. He realized that he finally had to stop asking, "Why is this happening to me?" and start asking, "How can God be glorified in this?"

I think he would say that he had to turn the tables and ask this question to protect his sanity. But the truth remains the same: when we begin and end the conversation by asking why something is happening to us instead of asking how God can use the situation for His good, we will always wrestle with accepting God as sovereign.

Why "God is Sovereign" is a BIG DEAL

There is a powerful reassurance. There is a great peace that can be tapped into when we realize that there is indeed someone in charge. We do not live in a random, chaotic, unknown, and pointlessly evolving universe. Those who have no room for a sovereign God are truly alone and adrift without an anchor or shelter from the storms of life.

There is a purpose and plan. God has a plan for His people and will carry it out (Judges 14:4; Psalm 138:8; Joel 3:16; Ephesians 1:5, 11). There is a reason for the ongoing struggles that we must endure.

Again, for peace and reassurance we read in Romans 8:28, "we know that in all things God works for the good of those who love Him," – but then we fail to include the vital truth in the following verse, "For those God foreknew He also predestined to *be conformed to the likeness of His Son*" (Romans 8:29).

God sovereignly works all things together for good, but His good is not always what we see as good. The good that God wants is being transformed into the likeness of His Son. *That* is the good that God is accomplishing in our lives.

There IS hope because God is sovereign. "For I know the plans I have for you," declares the Lord, "plans to prosper you and not to harm you, plans to give you hope and a future" (Jeremiah 29:11). It is only because God is sovereign that we can put our hope in Him.

God's sovereignty means we can put our trust in Him. His sovereign promises mean we do not always have to be as self-promoting and self-assertive as our human nature continually prompts us to be. We always make a statement about God when we act. We are born activists, which makes us poor waiters. "Heaven helps those who help themselves" is catchy phrase - but not a Biblical one.

When we feel the need to take control, we are often doing so at the expense of waiting on the Lord. The simple truth is, we do not have the autonomy that we think we have. God is in charge – not us.

God's sovereignty brings contentment. When we recognize that God is in charge and that His promises to us are real, we are more easily satisfied with what God has given or withheld from us. Envy is the denial of providence. When we desire things we do not have, we are in effect not accepting what God has sovereignly given to us.

"Inverted Christianity" is the practice of continually asking God to bless *our* plans and accomplish *our* goals and purposes.[8] It's having tunnel vision that is only focused on what we want instead of being open to God's will for us. A belief in a sovereign God allows us to be satisfied with God's plans and God's goals for us. Embracing God's sovereignty opens up our vision to a wider range of possibilities in which we can delight.

Crisis moments are orchestrated for a reason. In some ways, God is never really content with your spiritual growth and maturity. This is because His continual desire is for you to always grow closer to Him. When those moments arrive, when we are tempted to scream, "What is going on?!" we are then given the opportunity to actively trust in the sovereignty of God.

C.S. Lewis has noted that pain is God's megaphone; it's how He gets our attention.[9] This means that it's often to God's glory that we fail. In fact, it is often to God's glory that people experience hardship. Because when God sovereignly acts to get our attention, He does so for a good reason.

God's sovereignty protects us from a life of regrets. We all make mistakes. We all wish we could do things over. But when we realize God is sovereign, we can have a peace about mistakes of the past. God has already accounted and compensated for all of your missteps.

Was God happy that you robbed that liquor store when you were 13 years old? No, He wasn't. But He has allowed all of your mistakes for a reason. You never did anything that caught Him unaware. You have no reason to beat yourself up for past events; God let them occur for His purposes. Admittedly, this is very hard for us to fully understand.

This last point also comes with a word of caution: First, we can never use God's sovereignty as an excuse for our own shortcomings.

To say, "Well, I can't help it; God made me this way" doesn't work. Secondly, we can never allow this doctrine to cause us to react passively to the actions of others. Injustice and evil must be confronted. We are to be salt and light to a dying and decaying world. Lastly, we can never use God's sovereignty as an excuse for our own sinful actions. We are still accountable for the wrong things we have done, even if God is able to use them to accomplish His will.[10]

Reflection Questions:

1. What situation in your life has challenged your belief in the sovereignty of God?
2. Which mystery, unknown thing, or unanswered question do you wrestle with the most?
3. Do you think it's fair that God does what He pleases? Why or why not?
4. Why is it hard to accept the premise that God allows evil to accomplish His purposes?
5. In what situation do you need to turn the tables and ask how God can be glorified?
6. What is underlying your resistance to accept the sovereignty of God in your life?
7. Because God is sovereign, I will . . .

"Think-On-It" Verse:
"I am God, and there is none like Me. My purpose
will stand, and I will do all that I please."
Isaiah 46:9-10

"For as the Father has life in Himself, so He
has granted the Son to have life in Himself."
John 5:26

13 - God is Self-Existent

A Most Extraordinary Day

Long ago in a dusty wilderness, Moses found himself tending sheep, minding his own business, doing whatever it is that shepherds do, when he noticed something odd. A bush was on fire but was not being burned. Moments later, Moses found himself barefoot and having a conversation with God – and not just any conversation, but a conversation about freeing the Hebrew people from their slavery and the oppressive Egyptian rule of Pharaoh.

In this sandal-less, Holy Ground conversation, Moses asked God a fairly simple, straightforward, and totally reasonable question: "When I go to the Israelites and tell them, 'The God of your fathers has sent me to you,' and they ask me, 'What is His name,' What should I tell them?"

It was a fair question, but God's answer to Moses doesn't seem all that clear or satisfying. God answered with a simple, "I AM who I AM." Moses was told to tell anyone who asks, "I AM has sent me to you."

Now if I were Moses, I probably would have said something stupid like, "I am what!?" You can't just be an "I Am" – You have to be an "I am … *something!*" (Fill in the blank with 100 different things, like "I am the ALMIGHTY God!" then add a huge thunderclap and blinding light to drive the point home.)

It's easy to be a bit confused by the simple, "I AM who I AM" response. If I were Moses, I would have been standing there with my head cocked sideways thinking, "Huh?" (In fact, I would *still* be standing there with my head cocked sideways thinking, "Huh?")

The "I Am" answer, while somewhat ambiguous and confusing, is an answer with a richness and depth that we fail to fully understand at first glance. All other answers would have been limiting. This answer shows that God is unlimited. But this response also reveals that God is the great "I AM" – which means (among a whole host of other things) that God is self-existent.

A New Category of Thinking

The self-existent nature of God can be partially explained this way: every effect must have a first cause. By definition this is true. The problem is, God is not an effect. God has no beginning, which means He has no first (or antecedent) cause. Being eternal, He has within Himself the power of being. He needs no help from other sources to exist. Admittedly, this is a lofty and awe-inspiring concept. There is nothing else like it. Everything we see and know is dependent on a first cause. It is impossible for us to fully comprehend anything that is self-existent.[1]

We have a difficult time grasping this concept because it introduces us to a new category. Everything you own was created by someone or something. My pen was "created" in a plastic molding machine in Taiwan. A rock was created by God. Created things can then become creators. I made a lamp in my 7th grade shop class. But all creators were once created; all creators except God. Everything we see has been created by God, directly or indirectly.

God certainly makes us think outside the box in our efforts to understand His nature. This is especially true when we try to comprehend His self-existence. We all have an origin, a beginning, but God does not. God is self-caused, without beginning. The word *origin* applies only to created things and not to the eternal one who caused it all.[2]

Objections to a Self-Existent God

Like infinity and eternity, our minds have no way to process something as abstract as the concept of "not created." Even the most brilliant scientist with no room for God will still acknowledge that the things he sees through a telescope (or under a microscope) have a beginning. But it's more than just a challenge to our intellect; our hearts and our pride also wrestle with accepting the category of "non-created."

Our Minds

Our minds have a difficult time embracing this idea of anything existing without a beginning, without a start of some kind. We have no neat category into which we file this kind of God. We have an uneasiness about a supreme being without a beginning. It's new and totally different to our way of thinking. It's a bit unsettling to realize there is One who accounts to no one for His being. God is responsible to no one. This self-dependence and self-sufficiency is not just hard; it's impossible for us to understand.[3]

90

Our Hearts

Our pride also will not allow us to concede the simple fact that God has the right to claim self-existence, to not have a cause or a creator. Some might even find God arrogant to propose such a ludicrous idea. Everything must have a beginning. Who is God to exclude Himself from this necessity? Our hesitancy to fully accept God as self-existent due to our pride means that we have to admit there is one who exists beyond our ability to reason. It takes humility to do that – more than most of us are willing to concede. Our pride keeps our concept of God down on our own level. This way we can still manage Him, still have some measure of control over Him.[4]

Our Experience

Believers are not immune from failing to understand or fully appreciate a God without a starting point or a beginning. We seldom, if ever, let our minds dwell on this aspect of God for more than a fleeting moment. In some respects it's a sobering thought that we who live so entrenched in a Christian church culture and who may even work to promote and share our faith with others, may live our whole lives without ever seriously thinking about the great wonder of the "I AM" self-existence of God.[5]

If you want a God you can conceive, a self-existent one is not for you. But if you want a God who is fully and solely worthy of your worship, awe, and adoration, He must be the ultimate cause of everything.

A Necessity

The simple fact of the matter is that God must be self-existent; it is absolutely necessary for Him to be so. It's the only reasonable explanation for all that we see around us every day. To be intellectually honest, we must admit that all we see must have a first cause. The truth is, "something must have within itself the power of being. Otherwise there would be nothing. Unless something existed in itself, nothing could possibly exist at all."[6]

It's the ultimate chicken-or-the-egg question. For anything to exist, something must have first existed. All that we see needed to be started from something. It's impossible to get something from nothing. The self-existent God is the "something" that caused the "everything."

Why "God is Self-Existent" is a BIG DEAL

"So what if God has always existed?" "What does this do for me?" "What difference can this make in my life?" The answers to these questions are also found in that short, ambiguous, non-definitive answer given to Moses' question. The answers are found in the pointed reply of "I Am."

In Hebrew, "I Am" ('ehyeh) is translated and can be understood to mean "I will be." When you consider the context of the original conversation, Moses' upcoming challenges with Pharaoh, and the daunting task that lay ahead, "I will be with you" is what Moses heard God say. This is why Moses seemed unaffected by the answer that we find so ambiguous.

This name through which God revealed Himself was also a clear indication of God's promises and His help. The "I Am" name revealed something essential about His attributes and character.

The "I Am" reply implied that God is, "I am *anything* that you need Me to be." It is truly an unlimited answer. Anything else that God calls Himself would be seen as confining.

If God called Himself "Almighty," we would see Him as *only* Almighty. But He is much, much more than that. God did not want to define Himself with words which we would later use to limit Him.

God's self-existence is also further proof of His sovereignty and omnipotence. It shows us that He is also an eternal God, which gives us yet another facet to His transcendence. We see multiple attributes of God working together when we recognize the self-existence of God.

This deeper understanding of God gives us a more complete understanding of our problems. Because God created us and rules His universe providentially, it stands to reason that all of the solutions to our problems, trials, and issues are in fact theological in nature.

When we better our understanding of God (including His lack of a beginning), we have a more solid foundation of faith on which to build our lives. We then see our difficult circumstances in a different light. This alone makes the teaching of God's self-existent nature something practical, not just theoretical, dry, and boring.[7]

The more we know about God, the clearer our realization becomes of how He is at work in us. We recognize the purpose and plans He has for us. We then have the ability to put our faith and trust more fully in Him.

Reflection Questions:

1. If you were Moses, how would you have reacted at the burning bush conversation?
2. What do you need God to be for you today?
3. If you were God, how would you finish the "I Am..." statement?
4. What in you resists accepting the self-existence of God?
5. How is this quality seen in the life and person of Christ?
6. How does an atheist explain the ultimate origin of everything?
7. Because God is self-existent, I will ...

"Think-On-It" Verse:

"Before the mountains were born or You
brought forth the earth and the world, from
everlasting to everlasting You are God."
Psalm 90:2

"If you sin, how does that affect Him? If your sins are many, what does that do to Him? If you are righteous, what do you give to Him or what does He receive from your hand? Your wickedness affects only a man like yourself, and your righteousness only the sons of men."
Job 35:5-8

14 - God is Self-Sufficient

"God Does Not Need You"
How do you feel about such a blunt statement? A bit slighted? A bit insecure? A bit unappreciated? It is not a warm fuzzy thought, is it? It's not a concept we want to embrace or relish.

But the truth is, God does not need you. But think about it for a moment. What if the opposite were true? What if God *did* need us? Where would we be then?

It's sort of counterintuitive, but you might agree that it is a good thing, a very good thing, that God does not need us. Conversely, it's quite an unsettling thought to think that God would need us for anything.

When God revealed himself to Moses at the burning bush with the name, "I Am" He revealed three vitally important things about His character: 1.) He is self-existent; 2.) He is eternal; and 3.) He is self-sufficient.

For God to be God, by definition He must be self-sufficient. If God has any needs, it would mean He is incomplete, and that would mean He is not perfect. *Need* is a word that applies only to us, not to our Creator. God has a voluntary relationship with us. His desire for this relationship comes only from His sovereign good pleasure, not because we can supply Him with something He is lacking. He is complete, He is whole, and He is satisfied without us.[1]

We cannot have a God with needs. Unlike the gods of myth and folklore, our God has no needs to be appeased. He does not have to be made happy through our efforts.

Atheists Don't Ruin God's Day
When I read a book, I have a pen in hand so I can underline things I want to remember. Sometimes I'll use a highlighter pen or put a star in the margin next to something I think is really important. This next

paragraph in my copy of *The Knowledge of the Holy* is underlined, highlighted, and has a star in the margin. This quote may be the most challenging (and most troubling) one in this book.

> "Were every man on earth to become an atheist, it could not affect Him in any way. He is what He is in Himself without regard to any other. To believe in Him adds nothing to His perfections; to doubt Him takes nothing away."[2]

Are you kidding me? God would not be affected if everyone on the planet ignored or even denounced Him? This is impossible for us to fully understand because it's impossible for us to relate to. To some degree, everyone is a people pleaser. We all have a need to be liked. We all value others' opinions about ourselves. Not God. He is not like us. He has no need to be liked. His opinion about Himself is unaffected by our opinions or our actions toward Him.

God and His Emotions
This might be the most poignant example of how God is not like us. If everyone on the planet became an atheist, it would not ruin God's day. It would ruin our day. Imagine if no one showed up for church on a Sunday morning except the preacher. He would take it personally. He would feel badly about himself. He would have to wonder, "What did I do wrong?" It would negatively affect his view of himself. Evidently, if we all blew off church one Sunday, God would not feel the same way.

God is not like us. He does have and feel emotions. There are plenty of examples in the scriptures of God showing His emotions. He is a jealous God. He gets angry at sin. He can be grieved by our sinful actions. Jesus cried at the death of a friend. Our actions may have an influence on Him, but they do not affect the way He feels about Himself.

A Thick-Skinned God and Thin-Skinned People
Our emotions and our view of ourselves are most often tied to the opinions others have about us. We cannot project this experience of ours onto God. God is caring and sensitive, loving and personal, but He is also a thick-skinned God. Your opinion of Him does not hurt His feelings. He doesn't take it personally when we sin. Do you need to imitate this perspective of God's in your own life?

We need a healthy thick and thin-skinned balance. We are often too thin-skinned. We are often too easily offended. We can be easily hurt. We let others' opinions have a great influence on how we see ourselves. How do you react to insults, to not being invited to a party, to not being recognized at work?

There is a good chance your imitation of God's character may need to include not letting others' opinions of you (or actions towards you) affect how you feel about yourself. We often allow others' opinions to drag us down and discourage us. We need to live our lives before an audience of one: God.

Partners but Not a Partnership

When we say that God is Almighty, we need to stop and think about what the word *Almighty* actually means. It means that God does not need your help. Somehow we have fallen into the habit of thinking we enter into some sort of partnership with God, where we help Him out by serving Him. We never say it out loud, but we often have this inner sense that God needs us to do this or that for Him. When we think we are necessary to God, we fail to realize that God is not any greater because we are here and He would not be any less if we were not.[3]

It is by His voluntary choice, not by His need, that He asks us to come alongside Him and work in this world to accomplish His will. This is yet another mystery that we are left to ponder. He does not need our help with anything, but He allows us to be a part of advancing His plan on earth by being a blessing to others.

Three Great Points to Remember

Arthur Pink made three points about the self-sufficiency of God as seen in the following three quotes.[4]

> "During a past eternity, God was alone: self-contained, self-sufficient, self-satisfied; in need of nothing. Had a universe, had angels, had human beings been necessary to Him in any way, they also had been called into existence from all eternity."

God does not change, which means that our creation has not changed Him one bit. It has not added anything to Him; it has not made Him better; it has not completed Him or added anything to His glory.

> "God was under no constraint, no obligation, no necessity to create. That He chose to do so was purely a sovereign act on His part, caused by nothing outside of Himself, determined by nothing but His own good pleasure..."

If indeed God "works out everything in conformity with the purpose of His will" (Ephesians 1:11), then God created us simply because He wanted to, and for no other reason than that.

"God is no gainer even from our worship. He was in no need of that external glory of His grace that arises from His redeemed, for He is glorious enough in Himself without that."

God does not get "recharged" because we worship Him on Sunday. Our worship of Him is for our benefit, not His. If every church were empty and no notes were sung ever again, God would be unaffected by the deafening silence.

These three quotes may be stretching your concept of God in some pretty uncomfortable ways. But remember the only God that is worthy of our worship is a God that is bigger than the one we conveniently carry around with us in our thoughts. God must be like this because He is not like us.

Why "God is Self-Sufficient" is a BIG DEAL

What is the application of God's self-sufficiency for us? We benefit from this attribute in many ways.

Only a self-sufficient God is truly worthy of our trust. If God needs us, what does that say about our needs? If God has needs, He can't be the one who meets all of ours. God meets our needs with a pure love and pure motives. He does not provide for us in order to woo us, to win us over, nor in the hope that we will love Him more if He is good to us and gives us what we desire.

We should feel honored that God has asked us to come alongside Him in His work. "For we are God's workmanship, created in Christ Jesus to do good works, which God prepared in advance for us to do." (Ephesians 2:10). God does not need us to accomplish His will, but He has asked us to work with Him and through Him. In fact, according to this verse, He has predestined our good works.

If God cannot be affected by our behavior, He can never lose His love for us. No matter how sinful we become, no matter how much our lives may take on the look of the prodigal son, God will always love us as His children. Christ loved those who spit on Him and nailed Him to the cross because He was self-sufficient and was able to separate their actions from who they were. This is seen when He said,

> "Father, forgive them, for they do
> not know what they are doing."
> (Luke 23:34)

The opposite is also true; we should feel a reassurance and a deliverance from the pressure of having to earn God's love. God does not love you more because you put a couple of extra dollars in the offering plate. He does not love you more because you used your vacation time for a mission trip instead of a fishing trip with your buddies.

Only a self-sufficient God is worthy of your praise and adoration. It makes God bigger and more transcendent when you realize He has no needs like we do. It's harder to shrink Him down to something manageable and understandable when we realize His self-sufficiency.

God desires our obedience, not our sacrifice. Because God does not need anything, we cannot give Him anything that is not already His. God desires our hearts and our obedience, not the "things" or talents we can bring to Him.

> "Does the Lord delight in burnt offerings and
> sacrifices as much as in obeying the voice of
> the Lord? To obey is better than sacrifice."
> (1 Samuel 15:22)

Reflection Questions:

1. "God does not need you." How does that make you feel? Why?
2. What comfort can be found in the fact that God does not need us?
3. Why would we want a God who needs us?
4. What would actually happen if God did need us?
5. How do you fall into the trap of thinking that God needs your help to accomplish His will?
6. How does knowing this attribute affect your worship of God?
7. Because God is self-sufficient, I will . . .

"Think-On-It" Verse:

"The God who made the world and all things in it,
since He is Lord of heaven and earth, does not dwell
in temples made with hands nor is He served by human
hands as though He needed anything since He Himself
gives to all people life and breath and all things."
Acts 17:24-25

> "Praise be to the name of God for ever
> and ever; wisdom and power are His."
> Daniel 2:20

15 - God is Wise

Wisdom and Wrinkles?

When you hear the word *wisdom*, what's the first image that pops into your head? No pondering or deep thinking allowed. What's your first reaction to the word wisdom?

Do you think of a wrinkled old man with a long gray beard, sitting atop a mountain with his legs folded in his lap? This guru is seen by many as the example of wisdom personified. Often people think that Confucius and Buddha were wise because they supposedly were able to dispense advice to answer the deep and mysterious questions of life. Fortunately, wisdom is not a wrinkled old man.

Wisdom is Not . . .

Today we often confuse wisdom with intelligence. We think intelligent people must be wise because they're so smart. But the truth is, there are a lot very intelligent people who have accomplished many amazing things, but they still haven't shown much wisdom in how they live their lives.

Some of the smartest and most successful people on the planet have some of the worst marriages and family situations because they have made some very foolish decisions. Wisdom is **not** seen in how clever or how smart you are.

We can also confuse wisdom with knowledge. Knowledge and intelligence are certainly related, but knowledge specifically addresses *how much* you know. People with great knowledge know a lot of information. For example, university professors have great knowledge in their field of study.

But just because you have great knowledge doesn't mean you will always make wise choices and decisions. Wisdom is **not** seen in what or how much you know.

Wisdom Is . . .

The word *wisdom* is tied to another word – *decision*. You only show your wisdom (or lack thereof) by the decisions that you make. The movie character, Forrest Gump, was fond of saying "stupid is as stupid does." He was right; your actions alone show whether or not you are stupid.

The same can be said of wisdom. Your choices and your decisions show whether you are wise or foolish. You can be very smart and have great ability to figure things out – but still not be wise. You can have a lot of knowledge – but not act wisely with what you know. Forrest could also have said "wisdom is as wisdom does." Wisdom **is** seen in your actions.

His Wisdom is Seen in His Actions

God is omniscient; He knows everything. But His wisdom is not seen in this characteristic of being all knowing. It is seen in His actions toward us. God is wise in the actions He takes toward His creation.

So what does it mean to say that God is wise? His wisdom is best seen in His goals and how He goes about achieving them. This goes beyond the idea that God knows everything. It indicates that God's decisions about His actions are always wise and honoring to Himself. They will always bring about the best results; from God's perspective, not ours.[1]

God's wisdom is also seen in His continual action toward us in our daily lives. God is always at work. He is sovereignly orchestrating events behind the scenes, unknown to us most of the time. His wisdom is seen in His plans and in His will coming to fruition in the world around us. When this is truly understood, there is a peace available to the believer that brings relief and reassurance.[2] A wise God has a plan, and He is working that plan in your life right now. His plan revolves around building your character, not just providing you the comfort and security your flesh may be longing for.

The Ultimate Example of God's Wisdom

God's wisdom is revealed in His doing the best thing, in the best way, at the best time, for the best purpose. The ultimate example of God's wisdom is seen in His amazing plan of redemption found in the cross. Christ is "the wisdom of God" to those who believe, but foolishness to those who reject it and think of themselves as wise.[3]

> "Where is the wise person? Where is the teacher of the law?
> Where is the philosopher of this age? Has not God made
> foolish the wisdom of the world? For since in the wisdom
> of God the world through its wisdom did not know Him,
> God was pleased through the foolishness of what was preached

to save those who believe. Jews demand signs and Greeks look
for wisdom, but we preach Christ crucified: a stumbling block
to Jews and foolishness to Gentiles, but to those whom God
has called, Christ the power of God and the wisdom of God.
For the foolishness of God is wiser than human wisdom,
and the weakness of God is stronger than human strength."
(1 Corinthians 1:20-25)

We were first deceived by the serpent in the garden, but now we are
freed by the "foolishness" of God.[4]

Wisdom and the World
Many look around at our world today and seriously doubt or deny
God's wisdom. Those who believe God to be wise may be tempted to
defend His wisdom. This can be a real challenge, because recognizing
God's wisdom is a spiritual endeavor – not a mental one. Those who
make a choice not to believe would not be convinced by any proof,
but those who worship God need none.[5]

The recognition of God's wisdom is a spiritual experience, not a
mental exercise. You will rarely convince a non-believer that God is
wise; it must be shown to them through an illuminated heart and
mind.

To those who walk with God and abide with Him, the wisdom of God
is a non-debatable point; it's as obvious as the sun and gravity. Only
believers can fully recognize the infinite wisdom in an infinite God.

Wisdom and Worldly Common Sense
Wisdom and common sense have different goals. Common sense
focuses on the ways of the world. For example, Ben Franklin wrote:
"A penny saved is a penny earned." This piece of advice may help you
make good financial decisions.

But wisdom has a different focus. Wisdom conforms us to the ways of
heaven. Wisdom brings us spiritual blessings, not worldly comforts.
Wisdom leads us to view the world differently; it changes all that we
think is important to us and turns on its head what we think is
valuable.

> "Wisdom is a right understanding of the world and our role in it.
> It knows who God is, it knows who we are, and it sees the relative
> importance of all things. It is a correct ordering of priorities,
> majoring on truth and character before superficial pleasures. It is
> the only way, in the long run, to be truly satisfied."[6]

Wisdom and Relationship

Why do you want wisdom? Most want direction and information without submission, and divine guidance without any demands of our character. But gaining wisdom means getting God first. God is not an oracle giver; He is a life transformer. Wisdom is found in relationship with Christ, not in a crystal ball. The world seeks help and guidance in horoscopes, tarot cards, psychics, and fortune tellers because there is no accountability, submission, or demands that accompany them.

God is no different. It's tempting to take a utilitarian approach to God. Many only want God in their lives because they need His help and His direction. They want God's guidance as a means of self-improvement. But God is not a self-help technique; He is the lover of our souls, and no love relationship fulfills its purpose when one party selfishly uses the other for his own benefit.[7]

Why "God is Wise" is a BIG DEAL

We can trust His sovereign rule in this world. Because God is wise, we can fully put our faith and trust in Him and His continual actions. God is not learning on the job. He never agonizes over any decisions. His wisdom is seen in His providential care and orchestration of His will. He always accomplishes His purposes.

Trusting God is a factual exercise, not an emotional event. There is an inherent conflict between wisdom and our emotions. You will rarely feel wise. Your emotions, on the other hand, will lead you to all kinds of places. Trusting in the wisdom of God is a challenge for every believer. When you find yourself worrying, are you trusting in God's wisdom or letting your emotions dictate what is true?

God shares His wisdom with us. This is an attribute that we share with Him in some small way. We, the finite creatures of three-pound brains, *can* possess a measure of godly wisdom. When we seek it in our abiding relationship with Christ, it helps us navigate through this life. But as wise as you may become, your wisdom will always pale in comparison to the boundless and infinite wisdom of God.[8]

Obviously we can never be as wise and all knowing as God. We are limited in some very significant ways. But we do have more than enough access to the wisdom of God. His moral direction for our lives can easily be found in God's Word and the counsel of godly friends.

When we seek and find godly wisdom from His Word and good counsel, we are often protected from the self-inflicted troubles and disasters of our often superficial decisions. The "wisdom" of the world is ultimately self-destructive and self-defeating. Examples of this can be easily seen each and every day.

When we find ourselves walking in godly wisdom, sin is not something we need to overcome; it is something that largely becomes irrelevant. A wise believer can smoke all the marijuana he wants; it's just that he doesn't want to smoke any at all. Foolish behavior is seen as foolish. It has no draw; it has no temptation for those who are living and abiding in God's wisdom.

Wisdom is found in submission. We think we know best, but our decisions are too often based on our wants and our emotions. We often use God as our consultant instead of the driving force of our decisions. We ask Him to come alongside our plans and bless them instead of being truly open to His leading. But there is a far better option; it's to no longer solely rely on our own insight and discretion.

Wanting to know the future and wanting to plan well for our lives is a natural inclination for most. But in fact, insisting that things go according to our plan can be a real hindrance to our spiritual growth. God has made Himself fully responsible for us, and He stands ready to take over the management of our lives when we turn to faith in Him and submit to His will.[9]

Wisdom is found in refinement. Through the trials of life, we are conformed into the likeness of His Son (Romans 8:29). We grow in our wisdom and understanding as we gain a deeper knowledge of God through the difficult circumstances of life.

The Scriptures tell us that our trials are ultimately for our benefit. Our growing in wisdom is the result of spiritual maturity and completeness.

> "The testing of your faith produces perseverance.
> Let perseverance finish its work so that you may
> be mature and complete, not lacking anything."
> (James 1:3-4)

We must remember that our wisdom and understanding will always be limited. As we live and breathe on this planet, we will never fully share in God's wisdom. This means we will never fully understand why God allows some things to happen. There is a certain futility in constantly asking why. We need to stop trying to interpret the ways of God and start learning how we can live in deeper dependence on Him.

"The life you have constructed may be falling apart, but the life God has fashioned for you is not. His wisdom has known all things before the foundation of the world. If God has let you be undone, He has allowed it for a reason. He is bringing you to the end of your sinful self and to the beginning of life in His secure arms. Wisdom was appointed from eternity past, you are a latecomer. God is bringing you home."[10]

Wisdom is found in a promise. God promises to give us the wisdom that we need.

"If any of you lacks wisdom, he should
ask God, who gives generously to all without
finding fault, and it will be given to him."
(James 1:5)

Wisdom is found in fearing God. The Scriptures repeatedly tell us that wisdom is found in fearing God. "The fear of the Lord is the beginning of wisdom." (Psalm 111:10 and Proverbs 1:7; 9:10). When we fully realize that our poor decisions are dishonoring God, we are more likely to make wiser decisions. But when we are living to please only our flesh, unaware of the consequences of our disobedience, we are exhibiting a sincere lack of godly fear. But when we realize that the possibility of heavenly discipline exists, we are then far more likely to give credibility to God's commands.[11]

Wisdom is found in waiting patiently for God to speak. Sometimes it takes a while for us to hear from God for guidance and direction. It may be God's way of weeding out our own selfish desires. At other times it may be God's way to test our hearts. When God seems slow in speaking, we may be tempted to take matters into our own hands.

This was the downfall of King Saul in 1 Samuel 13:12. Saul could not wait any longer for God's priest to arrive, so he made the sacrifice himself – something he was not permitted to do. Like Saul, we may not think our action is an act of disobedience; we may reason that unanswered prayers mean God wants us to act. He doesn't. He may be waiting to see what's more important to us – our obedience or our survival.[12]

Waiting for God to speak is hard, frustrating and sometimes even scary. But waiting for God to speak is important for us to do. God speaks, and God promises to give us wisdom, but not always according to our schedule and time frame. Be careful not to cheat yourself out of God's blessings by taking matters into your own hands.

Reflection Questions:

1. Do you ever find yourself doubting the wisdom of how God works in this world? When?
2. Do you ever find yourself doubting the wisdom of how God works in your life? When?
3. How does doubting or questioning His wisdom affect your relationship with Him?
4. Do you recognize the foolishness of questioning God's wisdom or are you still doubting?
5. Even when you acknowledge God's wisdom, why is sin still a struggle rather than something irrelevant to you?
6. List some examples of godly wisdom conflicting with worldly common sense.
7. Because God is wise, I will . . .

"Think-On-It" Verse:

"Oh, the depth of the riches of the wisdom and knowledge of God! How unsearchable His judgments, and His paths beyond tracing out! 'Who has known the mind of the Lord? Or who has been His counselor?'"
Romans 11:33-34

"I will lead the blind by ways they have not known, along unfamiliar paths I will guide them; I will turn the darkness into light before them and make the rough places smooth. These are the things I will do; I will not forsake them."

Isaiah 42:16

16 - God is Faithful

A Heart Challenge

When you read that God is infinite, your brain is stretched to try to understand what that means. The same is true for His omniscience, omnipotence, omnipresence, transcendence, and some of His other hard-to-fathom attributes. It is a *mental* challenge to understand these characteristics of God.

But the phrase, God is faithful, challenges us in another way. It's not that we wrestle *mentally* with the concept of His faithfulness, but rather we face the challenge of *feeling* it to be true in our hearts. This is not an intellectual concept to figure out; this is an emotional issue.

Why? Because after you read God is faithful, about three whole nanoseconds elapse before you start to doubt and wonder if this is *really* true. This happens because we have all felt the exact opposite from time to time. We have all been disappointed. We have all had prayers go unanswered. We have all been confused by His actions. This one is an issue of the heart, not the brain.

Are Faith and Trust Dying Words?

Do you lock your car when you go into the grocery store? Is your home locked when you are away? Why? We don't have faith in others like we used to. We lock everything up because we're afraid someone will steal our stuff. We don't trust each other very much these days.

We expect and even accept unfaithfulness as a part of life. When it kills a marriage, there is no shame; it's just a sad or unfortunate thing. In fact, we actually find marital unfaithfulness a source of entertainment in various TV shows and movies. What used to grieve us as a society is increasingly permitted and accepted, if not lauded, by some. In some measure, our culture even celebrates unfaithfulness.

The Unfaithfulness Bleed-Over

The problem is this: our rampant unfaithfulness with each other then bleeds over into our relationship with God. We have no experience with true faithfulness, so we find it hard, if not impossible, to see God as being faithful. But in spite of *our* broken promises to one another, God is faithful to His promises. His faithfulness means that He will always fulfill what He has promised. We can rely on Him; He will never be unfaithful to those who trust in what He has said. This is the essence of true faith: taking God at His word and relying on Him to do what He has promised.[1]

Throughout this book, there have been repeated warnings about the danger of imposing your own experiences onto God by assuming that He sees and reacts to things in the same way you do. The same can be said here. Just because others have broken their promises, don't assume that God has also broken His promises to you.

What Has God Promised You?
It may be obvious, but still necessary to point out, that God is faithful to fulfill His promises. He is never bound to give us our wants, desires, or even our every need for that matter. When you think back over your own disappointments in life that have eroded your belief that God is faithful, was God breaking His promises or simply not fulfilling your wants?

What has God promised you? This is a question that you are going to have to explore and answer on your own. You may be surprised by the answers that you find. God has not promised you many of the things that you might find yourself hoping and praying for.

God Has Promised Us Trouble and Trials
God has never promised us an easy life – quite the opposite; He has promised us times of trial and suffering.

> "I have told you these things, so that in Me you
> may have peace. In this world you will have trouble.
> But take heart! I have overcome the world."
> (John 16:33)

God has never promised you peace apart from Him. He allows, and in fact may even orchestrate, difficult circumstances in your life, but always with the purpose of growing your character in Christlikeness and drawing you closer to Himself.

God Has Promised to Grow and Stretch Us
God is faithful to grow mature believers. *That* is His job – not to provide the blessings and comfort we all long for. Take the time to read the following passages for a better understanding of how God

works to grow us in our maturity and faith (2 Samuel 21:15; Psalm 66:10; Romans 4:18-25; 1 Thessalonians 5:24).

A demonstration is needed from time to time to show that our faith is indeed in God and not in what God has given to us. Times of trouble and trial are the way God stretches us to test this faith. God tries our faith in order for us to try His faithfulness.

> "Though now for a little while you may have had to suffer
> grief in all kinds of trials. These have come so that your
> faith – of greater worth than gold, which perishes even though
> refined by fire – may be proved genuine and may result
> in praise, glory and honor when Jesus Christ is revealed."
> (1 Peter 1:6-7)

As the Book of Job begins, it was God who pointed out to Satan the faithfulness of Job. Satan was not the one who brought Job into the conversation; it was God who initiated the sequence of events that would soon befall His faithful servant. If Job had his way, I'm sure he would rather have been left out of this conversation altogether, but Job was chosen to be a demonstration for us – so we can see God's glory and purpose displayed.

Faith, Doubt and Pessimism
We see doubt as the enemy to faith, but doubt isn't always such a bad thing. It may even serve a useful purpose in our lives. In *The Reason for God*, Timothy Keller pointed out the benefits of doubt:

> "A faith without some doubts is like a human body without
> antibodies in it. People who blithely go through life too busy or
> indifferent to ask hard questions about why they believe what they
> do will find themselves defenseless against either the experience of
> tragedy or the probing questions of a smart skeptic. A person's
> faith can collapse almost overnight if she has failed over the years
> to listen patiently to her own doubts, which should only be
> discarded after long reflection."[2]

Something has to grow our spiritual muscles stronger. *Something* has to give our faith strength to endure. Living a life of comfort and ease makes us soft; our doubts and difficulties can actually grow us stronger in our faith and closer to the Lord.

While doubt may serve a productive purpose, pessimism does not. God is glorified by our expectation of His faithfulness.

> "It is a strange dynamic to human eyes: Those who have never
> seen or expected God's blessings will never receive it, while those
> who have will receive more. Does this seem unfair? It isn't.

Pessimism about God is faithlessness, and God does not honor faithlessness, He honors faith. Faith sees God for who He is before He has proven it yet again."[3]

God Has No Choice But to Be Faithful
In light of His other attributes of love, holiness, goodness, wisdom, and unchangeableness, it is God's very nature to be faithful. He simply cannot be unfaithful. By definition, God would cease to be God if He lied or did not live up to His promises. Again, it's another all-or-nothing proposition – either God is faithful or He is not God. He cannot act out of character with Himself.[4]

God really has no choice but to be faithful to His promises. You might not feel like He is faithful; you may focus on the waves of doubt. But God is faithful to His people because He has to be.

Although at times our circumstances may tempt us to think otherwise, God is faithful. Much like infinity and eternity, His faithfulness to us is also hard to fully understand.

"Far above all finite comprehension is the unchanging faithfulness of God. Everything about God is great, vast, incomparable. He never forgets, never fails, never falters, never forfeits His word. To every declaration of promise or prophecy the Lord has exactly adhered, every engagement of covenant or threatening He will make good…"[5]

The Scriptures speak to this fact:

"God is not a man, that He should lie, nor a son of man,
that He should change His mind. Does He speak and
then not act? Does He promise and not fulfill?"
(Numbers 23:19)

God is Faithful Regardless of Our Blessings
It is tempting to compile a list of examples of God's faithfulness (both in the Scriptures and in the history of the Church) in an effort to convince you that God is faithful to His promises, but God's faithfulness cannot be proven on a scale. We cannot list examples of His faithfulness on one side of the scale to show that they outweigh examples of His supposed unfaithfulness on the other side of the scale.

His faithfulness can never be proven because our circumstances will always challenge us to think otherwise. But even this is a part of God's design and purpose in our lives. Oswald Chambers wrote of this in his well known daily devotional, *My Utmost for His Highest*. On October

23rd he wrote about how God's design is for us to have a trust in Him regardless of our blessing. So much so that He will remove our blessings from us in order to gain our whole heart and our sole devotion.

"When we are born again, the Holy Spirit begins to work His new creation in us, and there will come a time when there is nothing remaining of the old life. Our old gloomy outlook disappears, as does our old attitude toward things. How are we going to get a life that has no lust, no self-interest, and is not sensitive to the ridicule of others? How will we have the type of love that 'is kind . . . is not provoked, and thinks no evil'? (1 Corinthians 13:4-5).

The only way is by allowing nothing of the old life to remain, and by having only simple, perfect trust in God; *such a trust that we no longer want God's blessings, but only want God Himself. Have we come to the point where God can withdraw His blessings from us without our trust in Him being affected?* Once we truly see God at work, we will never be concerned again about the things that happen, because we are actually trusting in our Father in heaven, whom the world cannot see."[6]

The hard question that we all must ask is this: Is your view of God's faithfulness dependent on His blessings? And if your answer is yes, can you see why God would remove these blessings from your life? A belief in God's faithfulness means nothing until one lacks the things they think they need. A belief in God's strength means nothing until one is completely helpless.[7]

God is Faithful Only If . . .
When we say God is faithful only if this or that happens in my life, then we are the ones who are dictating the situation and the result. We are never in the position of deciding whether or not this is a true characteristic and attribute of God based solely on our circumstances.

We are to live in hope, with an expectation that things will work out (Romans 8:28), but also fully realizing that things do not always work out the way we want them to. At this point, we are told to trust in God. This is why having God as a loving Father is so important.

Paul Tripp wrote on the importance of trusting in our Abba during times of confusion and doubt. He wrote of having to reassure his own children of their need to trust in him and how that same trust then carries over to our trust in a heavenly Father.

"I am going to ask you to do something – trust Daddy. When you walk down the hallway to do what Daddy has asked you to do, say to yourself, 'My Daddy loves me. My Daddy would never ask me to do anything bad. I am going to trust my Daddy and stop trying to be the Daddy of my Daddy.'"

"God does the same thing with you, over and over again. He meets you in one of the most difficult hallways of your life, kneels down before you in condescending love, and asks you to trust in His loving and wise rule, even though you don't have a clue what He is doing. He knows there are many times when your life doesn't look like there is anyone ruling it, let alone someone wise and good. He knows there will be times when you will wish you could write your own story. He knows that at times you will be overwhelmed by what is on your plate. He knows that His plan will confuse and confound you. And He knows the real test is found in trust. So He is willing to have the conversation with you over and over again, and He has made sure that His Word assures you of His rule again and again."[8]

Our Response to a Faithful God

It is important that we do more than just accept the fact that God is faithful; it is also necessary for us to do something in response to it. Our actions and our emotions should be affected by the promise of God's faithfulness. We as believers and followers of God should be the most optimistic and hopeful people on the planet because God is faithful.

Far too often, believers are some of the most pessimistic people you will ever find. It is a sobering commentary that many ungodly people cruise through this life with a more optimistic perspective than those who walk in daily fellowship with a faithful God.

When we are confused and challenged and when things don't make much sense to us, God reminds us that they don't have to. We are not the ones in charge; God is. Our understanding of why things happen as they do is not key to the operation of the universe.[9] We participate in it without being in control or knowing why things happen. This was God's message to Job at the conclusion of the book.

When we think we are the ones in control and think we have the right to manage our lives as we like, God may have to remind us that it is simply not our right, not our job, nor our responsibility; it's His. Our job is to simply trust a loving God and live in dependence, knowing His plans are for our best and that they will accomplish His will in our lives.

Why "God is Faithful" is a BIG DEAL

Because God is faithful... we can trust Him and His plans in the most difficult situations. He promises to *walk* with us through the valley of the shadow of death. Our problem is we want to *run*. All we want is for our problems to go away. God has other plans – to deliver us *through* trial, not *from* trial.

We often assume that our interests and God's interests automatically coincide; they do not. His plan for us is most often very different from our earthly wants and desires.

Because God is faithful... we can now better understand His purposes. He is more concerned about your character than your comfort. Easy lives leave us spiritually weak. Easy lives bring Him no glory. We all know that godly character is built when we walk with Him in faith through the trials of life.

The overarching purpose of the universe is not our comfort. God does not exist for our benefit; we exist for His. God's actions in our lives are not guided primarily for our welfare, but for His glory.

Because God is faithful... we can experience His peace and reassurance. Our fight (and it is a battle) is to put our trust in Him. This is not easy, but it can happen when we keep our thoughts and our focused attention on Him and not our circumstances (Philippians 4:6-8, 12-13).

Because God is faithful... we can have a bigger and wider perspective on our lives. His faithfulness is seen in big chunks of time. It's not so easily recognized in days or weeks or even months. Only by stepping back and seeing a wider perspective will we recognize God's faithfulness.

God slowly unrolls the scroll of our lives. Much has been unrolled, and each day a little bit more is made known, but there is so much more yet to be revealed to us. God is faithful to only show you the present. Our responsibility is to be faithful with what is known to us and to trust Him for what is unknown to us.

Because God is faithful... we can give up our desire for control. Having a feeling of control brings a feeling of security, but the truth is, life is out of control; that's His plan. The things we think will give us control end up controlling us, but when we realize that God is indeed faithful two things happen.

First, we are willing to live by His agenda and not our own. We are then willing to let Him be the boss. We are able to be servants of a loving master.

Secondly, we are then more willing to have a "treasure transfer" and value the things He values over the things we think are important. This is seeking first the kingdom of God (Matthew 6:33). Recognizing God's faithfulness allows this to happen.

Reflection Questions:

1. Generally, do you trust people or are you a bit more skeptical of others?
2. How have you seen God's faithfulness in action?
3. What situations has God used to test your concept of His faithfulness?
4. What has God promised you?
5. Are you willing to give up control of your life? What makes that hard?
6. What lingering doubts do you have that can actually be used to strengthen your faith?
7. Because God is faithful, I will . . .

"Think-On-It" Verse:
"Because of the Lord's great love we are not consumed,
for His compassions never fail. They are new
every morning; great is Your faithfulness."
Lamentations 3:22-23

"'Why do you call Me good?' Jesus answered.
'No one is good except God alone.'"
Luke 18:19

17 - God is Good

Your Local Bookstore Can Be a Depressing Place

The next time you're at the local bookstore, be careful where your eyes wander. I'm not talking about the adult reading section; I'm talking about the religious studies section. Even the best mood can easily be shattered by simply surveying the book titles of popular religious writings. Among the shelves you will see books titled, *God is Not Good, God is Not Great: How Religion Poisons Everything, Good without God,* and *The God Delusion.*

There's a lot of anti-God conversation out there. And even if one does believe in God, His goodness is certainly up for debate. Generations past may have questioned God's goodness, but this present culture is more apt to flat out deny it and even argue vehemently against it.

Good and the Very Standard of Good

In spite of what the local bookstore shelves say, God is good. He is and has been eternally predisposed to be kind, tender, full of goodwill, sympathetic, and unfailing in His attitude toward us and our sin. It is His very nature to bless us, and He takes great pleasure in the happiness of His people. God's goodness can be seen and taught throughout the Scriptures. But it's also something that must be accepted as an article of faith.[1]

God's goodness is closely tied to His sovereignty in that it affects everything that He does. Of God's providence J. I. Packer wrote:

"(It is) the unceasing activity of the Creator whereby, in overflowing bounty and goodwill, He upholds His creatures in ordered existence, guides and governs all events, circumstances, and free acts of angels and men, and directs everything to its appointed goal, for His own glory....God's providence is His constant care for and absolute rule over all His creation for His own glory and the good of His people."[2]

God is concerned with two things: His own glory and our own good. Because of this, He will never be stingy with those who are generous to Him. It goes against His character to do so.

Wayne Grudem explains the goodness of God with a different twist by adding,

> "The goodness of God means that God is the final standard of good, and that all God is and does is worthy of approval."[3]

In effect, God is also the final standard of His goodness. We always wrestle with who gets to define what is good. Who gets to decide what actions are worthy of approval? It may be good for me to get a new television – but not good for you if I stole it from your home.

But we are not the ones who get to make this ultimate decision. God is the final standard of good.[4] This then answers the thorny question of who gets to decide what is good. What if my "good" differs from yours? Not only is God good; He also defines what is good. It's not our job to decide what is good and what is bad; God has already laid down those foundations for us.

A Goodness that is Easy to See

Contrary to what many might think, God does not hide His goodness from us. It is plain to see when people are willing to recognize it. Arthur Pink points out that the goodness of God is seen quite easily in at least three things: His creation, His immediate mercy, and ultimately in His sacrifice of the cross.

First, creation displays God's goodness. It emanates from Him like the heat and light of the sun. On cloudy days we may not see the sun, but we know it is always there, undiminished. All that emanates from God is good.

> "God saw all that He had made and it was very good."
> (Genesis 1:31)

This goodness of God was seen first in creation. The more we learn of creation, the more the good and loving nature of the Creator becomes apparent.[5] We as image bearers are the highest of God's earthly creation. That is why we can praise God and say,

> "I am fearfully and wonderfully made; Your
> works are wonderful, I know that full well."
> (Psalm 139:14)

God's goodness is revealed in every sunset, every field of wild daises, every giant sequoia, and every playful sea otter. Only a fool would see these things and have the gall to utter, "God is not good."

Secondly, God's goodness is witnessed to in the immediate mercies we enjoy every minute of every day. Creation was not just a one-time event. God continues to create and sustain His very good creation as a testimony of His goodness to us.[6]

Like most people, I hate being sick. When I get the flu, it's a miserable experience for me *and* my entire family. But the one thought I always have when I'm lying there in all my misery is this: it really is amazing how well our bodies work almost all of the time. We don't appreciate the general goodness of God and the magnificence of our working bodies until we are sick. Then we lie there complaining and wondering how a loving God could ever allow us to feel this way.

Thirdly, God's goodness to us is seen in His patience with us.
"When man transgressed the law of his Creator, a dispensation of unmixed wrath did not at once commence."[7]

In Genesis 3:15, after the fall of man, God immediately promised that another would come and "crush the head of the serpent," referring to the ultimate goodness of God which would be witnessed at the cross.

I've said it before, all of God's attributes work together, and many of them are closely related to one another. God's goodness is the fuel for many of His other attributes such as His mercy, grace, and patience.
"God's mercy is His goodness toward those in distress, His grace is His goodness toward those who deserve only punishment, and His patience is His goodness toward those who continue to sin over a period of time."[8]

God is Good – Not Fantastic!! and Stupendous!!
We live in a world where we are constantly bombarded with advertising. Buy this! Shop here! You need one of these! We can be easily overwhelmed and then desensitized to all of these amazing claims. But God is not like that. He advertises Himself in refreshing and startling simplicity. God is good.
"His attitude toward us is good, His will toward us is good, and His works on our behalf are good. We are unaccustomed to pure forms in our world – everything is tainted with corruption – but with God, no superlative is necessary. From every angle we look at Him, we see goodness."[9]

Questioning God's Goodness
Only a few pages into the Scriptures, we see Adam and Eve wondering about God's goodness. This was because Satan's very first act was to openly question the goodness of the Creator. This doubt led to their sinful decision and the fall of man. Today, Satan no longer needs to

say these words to us; we speak them to ourselves. We question God's goodness because we do not trust Him as we should.

We live in a fallen world as fallen beings, but we need to be careful not to let our minds dwell too long on questioning God's goodness.

> "To question the goodness of God is, in essence, to imply that man is more concerned about goodness than God is ... To suggest that man is kinder than God is to subvert the very nature of God ... It is to deny God; and this is precisely the thrust of temptation, to question the goodness of God."[10]

Do you have that much audacity? Are you willing to say that you are more concerned about God's creation than He is? Hopefully not. But we do need to recognize two things: First, it's nothing short of an act of arrogance to openly question God's goodness and His motives. Secondly, at the core all of our sin is born out of doubting God's goodness.

Our Definition of Good is at Times Very Different from God's

Our good is almost always defined by what we think is good for *us*. His definition of good is whatever brings Him glory. These are most often two very different things.

In *Forgotten God*, Francis Chan tells a story about a visit to a sick man in the hospital. His condition was serious enough that he asked Chan and the elders at the church to come and pray for his healing. Before they prayed, Francis asked, "Why do you want to be healed?"[11]

I wish I was there to see the man's face. "Why do I want to be healed?!" It's like asking someone, "So explain to me again why you want to win the $50 million lottery jackpot?" Some answers seem too obvious. I don't know what the man said, but I certainly know what I would have said. I would have babbled on about my kids and my wife and my family and all the stuff I still wanted to do. All of these are good answers, but not the best answer.

The best answer, the answer Chan was looking for was something like, "I want to glorify God with my life, and there's more for me to do for Him." That answer shows a concern for God's glory and *His* good over our version of what is good. Our good would be to live, but God's good may be to use our death to somehow bring more glory to Himself. If we never take hold of this concept, we will always wrestle with the goodness of God. We will always see things as good or bad from our perspective, not God's.

Why "God is Good" is a BIG DEAL

Creation has its roots in God's goodness. It is the primary drive responsible for all the daily blessings He bestows on us each day. He created us because it felt good in His heart to do so. He then redeemed us on the cross for the same reason.[12]

Because God is good, we have no reason to be afraid, even as we fear Him. God is great, and this greatness should arouse a godly fear in us. But God is also good. And because of this goodness, we do not have to be afraid. "To fear Him – yet not be afraid" is a powerful and prevalent paradox in our Christian faith.[13]

Only when we recognize that God is good are we able to "give thanks in all circumstances" (1 Thessalonians 5:18). When we doubt and question God's good nature, we continually wrestle with the difficult situations of life. When we resolve ourselves to the fact that God is good, life immediately gets easier to handle.

When we recognize that "God is the definition and source of all good, we will realize that God Himself is the ultimate good that we seek."[14] Not understanding that God is good will keep us from seeking Him, while recognizing that God is indeed good will keep us running hard after Him.

Finally, when we realize that God is good, we are motivated to live a life that imitates that goodness. This happens in two ways:

First, by doing good to others.

> "Let us do good to all people, especially to
> those who belong to the family of believers."
> (Galatians 6:10)

Because God is good, we are to live lives marked by servanthood and sacrificial living. God's demeanor toward us is to be reflected in our attitude and actions toward others.

Second, our desire for Him is intensified by the belief that He is good.

> "Every good and perfect gift is from above,
> coming down from the Father of the heavenly Lights,
> who does not change like shifting shadows."
> (James 1:17)

There is no shadow or darkness to God. There is no evil in His being, He is only good. That is why He is described as the Father of Lights.[15]

We as believers in the infinitely good Father of Lights are to live our lives as children of light. The goodness of God motivates us to live lives very differently than those who live in darkness.

Reflection Questions:

1. What is your very first impression? Do you see God as good? Why or why not?
2. What would you say to someone who does not think God is good?
3. What would happen if God were not good?
4. What do you think about the Francis Chan story?
5. What are you saying if indeed you do openly question God's goodness?
6. Do you agree that all sin is born out of doubting God's goodness? Explain.
7. Because God is good, I will . . .

"Think-On-It" Verse:

"If you, then, though you are evil, know how to give good gifts to your children, how much more will your Father in heaven give good gifts to those who ask Him!"
Matthew 7:11

> "Be kind and compassionate to one another, forgiving
> each other, just as in Christ God forgave you."
> Ephesians 4:32

18 - God is Forgiving

Our Reasons for Running

There are only a few perfectly good and acceptable reasons why anyone should ever find themselves running; one is sports (exercise). If you are in an athletic competition or if you enjoy exercising, feel free to enjoy a good run. But for most of us, running in not a very natural or dignified thing to do. I once saw my mother run during a softball game, and I've never been able to look at her the same since.

The only other good reason to run is fear. If an adult is running and they're not participating in a sporting event, then something is terribly wrong. In almost every case these people are running *away* from something bad – a burning building, a bear, a man with a gun, a bear with a gun. People may also run to rescue others when they are in danger, but even this is a result of fear for the other person.

The Day God Ran

The parable of the prodigal son includes a scene we need to forever remember.

> "But while he was still a long way off, his father saw
> him and was filled with compassion for him; he *ran* to
> his son, threw his arms around him and kissed him."
> (Luke 15:20)

This then introduces a third acceptable reason for running: anticipation. When walking is just not fast enough, we may find ourselves running towards a loved one. This was the case for the father who ran to forgive his son. He did not saunter, amble, or mosey. He ran.

Obviously, we are the prodigal son and God is the father who forgives. What Jesus was saying is not complicated. When we repent, God runs to forgives us. He desires for the broken fellowship to be restored – so much so that He does not walk. He runs.

Our Pride and a Forgiving God

People often reject God because He is righteous, which means He judges right from wrong. Many reject Him because they can never fully understand His eternal nature. Many never accept the idea of a sovereign being who rules all, knows all, can do all, and is everywhere all at once. Many find these attributes hard-to-swallow, so they simply reject a belief in Him.

But strangely enough, even a forgiving God is hard for many people to believe in. And who wouldn't want to believe in a forgiving God? To most, it's His "best" attribute. But the truth is, even an all-forgiving God is difficult for many to believe in for two reasons, and they both have to do with our pride.

First, pride keeps many from acknowledging their sin. Non-believers see no need of a God who forgives because they think they have no need for one. To acknowledge their need of a forgiving God is to acknowledge their sin and a debt that is then owed.

And if that debt is paid, they then owe God something in return. Their fear is that they no longer can call the shots or be their own boss. They would then serve and be beholden to this God who saved them from their sins. Their pride fuels their independence and desire to serve only themselves.

Secondly, even Christians can easily have a tainted view of what a forgiving God is all about. We can ask God to forgive us of our sins; we can believe the sacrifice of Christ has washed our sins away; we can even believe we are in a right standing with God; but we still can have this feeling that we need to do *something* to keep earning His forgiveness.

It's hard for us to believe that we don't have to do *something* else – that indeed we *can't* do anything else. This is also an act of pride because in effect it's saying that Christ's sacrifice was not enough to keep our right standing with God, so we must add to it by doing good works and by living a holy life.

This isn't just an innocent misunderstanding; it's a self-righteous act to want to add your good works to the cross. It cheapens the work of Christ and keeps us in bondage by not fully realizing the amazing work of grace at the cross of Christ. You have been forgiven; the price for your sin has been paid.

Two Types of Forgiveness

There are two kinds of forgiveness that we experience from God: "One Day, Judge Forgiveness" and "Everyday, Dad Forgiveness."

"One Day, Judge Forgiveness" allows us our eternal salvation. We are born separated from God because of Adam and Eve's disobedience. As a result, the inheritance we all receive is sin and separation from God.

> "Just as sin entered the world through one man, and death through sin, and in this way death came to all men, because all sinned."
> (Romans 5:12)

Through Adam sin entered the world. This passed-on sin is known as inherited sin. Just as we inherit physical characteristics from our parents, we inherit our sinful nature from Adam. When our inherited sin is not forgiven, we spend eternity suffering the consequences (Matthew 25:46; John 3:36).

Even if you wanted to deny this inheritance, you could never deny the fact that we all fall short and sin every day. Ecclesiastes 7:20 says, "There is not a righteous man on earth who does what is right and never sins." 1 John 1:8 says, "If we claim to be without sin, we deceive ourselves and the truth is not in us."

This "One Day, Judge Forgiveness" happens on the day you ask God to forgive you of your sins. At that moment, He pours His righteousness into you and makes you holy. *From this one day forward,* you are promised eternal life because your sins have been atoned for, forgiven by God. The ultimate judge has declared you forever not guilty!

"Everyday, Dad Forgiveness" has *nothing* to do with our salvation, but it has everything to do with our continuing fellowship with God. Sin acts as interfering static in the relationship between the believer and God. Our daily sins do not break or sever the relationship, but they do interfere and interrupt it in significant ways. Our unconfessed sin makes it much harder to hear His voice, sense His leading, experience His peace, feel His presence, and share in His joy.

This is why it is important that we continually ask our Father to forgive us of these sins every day – not to ensure our salvation – but to keep our relationship with Him growing. Our salvation is set and never in question – we are clean and acceptable in His sight.

> "You are already clean because of the word I have spoken to you. Remain in Me, and I will remain in you."
> (John 15:3-4)

But we are cheating ourselves out of the intimacy of our fellowship with Christ when we have known, unconfessed sin in our lives.

God is our father, who we can then stay in fellowship with through this continual forgiveness of sin. "Everyday Dad Forgiveness" does *not* ensure our salvation; it does *not* keep our right standing before God; but it does allow us to continue in an abiding daily relationship with Him.

God is a forgiving God – so much so that He runs to forgive us when we repent, both on that one day when we were saved and every day afterwards. God will always run to forgive, no matter the ugliness of what we might have done.

> "If we confess our sins, He is faithful and just and will forgive us our sins and purify us from all unrighteousness."
> (1 John 1:9)

Why "God is Forgiving" is a BIG DEAL

Forgiveness is forever entwined with the words *relationship* and *holiness*. We can have no relationship with God if our sins are never confessed and forgiven. We cannot have a growing fellowship with Him when known and unconfessed sin is a part of our lives. God created us for relationship. Only the forgiving nature of God makes it possible for us to continue in relationship with Him.

Forgiveness brings freedom from our past. We have all sinned. When we fail to recognize the forgiveness of God for what we have done, we feel as if we are not truly forgiven Women may carry around the guilt of an abortion and men may carry around the guilt of an affair even after making a full confession of their sin to God and others. This happens when we don't fully understand this attribute of God's forgiveness. (This also may be the result of not fully understanding the extent of both God's grace and mercy.)

God is always bigger than our sin. We can always come to Him in repentance for the things that we have done. Scripture testifies to this great promise and truth in many places.

> "But where sin increased, grace increased all the more."
> (Romans 5:20)

> "Neither height nor depth, nor anything else in all creation, will be able to separate us from the love of God."
> (Romans 8:39)

Forgiveness frees us from legalism. Legalism leads us to believe that God's plan did not work, so now we have to add our own effort to it in order to be truly forgiven. The problem is that our good works are an attempt to pay off a debt with the wrong kind of currency. We owe a spiritual debt, and spiritual debts need to be paid for by a spirit being, not by you and your physical effort.

Forgiveness brings justice. How do you feel when you've been wronged or sinned against? We want things to be made right, we want justice, we want to get even. But when we have done wrong to another, we have a radically different view of the situation. We want mercy; we want forgetfulness.

The sense of fairness we desire was assumed by God Himself and poured out on Christ at the cross. We are no longer entitled to it. God declared once and for all that justice is His, not ours. Because we have been forgiven of our sins, we are now able to forgive others when they sin against us.

Forgiveness leads us to praise, love and adore the forgiver. Jesus once forgave a sinful woman while at a dinner party with some Pharisees. She soaked His feet with her tears and poured expensive perfume on Him while the Pharisees did what they did best – judged the woman.

> "Do you see this woman? I came into your house. You did not
> give Me any water for My feet, but she wet My feet with her tears
> and wiped them with her hair. You did not give Me a kiss, but this
> woman, from the time I entered, has not stopped kissing My feet.
> You did not put oil on My head, but she has poured perfume on My
> feet. Therefore, I tell you, her many sins have been forgiven – for
> she loved much. But he who has been forgiven little loves little."
> (Luke 7:44-47)

The fact that we are forgiven of our sins fuels our passion and our worship of God. We live in a state of adoring Him because He has done what we could never do – forgive our spiritual debt.

A Third Type of Forgiveness – "Every Day, Friend Forgiveness."
There is actually a third kind of forgiveness - the forgiveness we grant one another. Because God is forgiving by nature, we must also be willing to forgive when we are wronged. Forgiveness is something we receive from God, but it is also something we extend to others.

This is not an option, or something we are to strongly consider. It is a command given by Christ Himself.

> "And when you stand praying, if you hold
> anything against anyone, forgive him, so that your
> Father in heaven may forgive you your sins."
> (Mark 11:25)

Three Roles of Forgiveness: Judge, Dad and Friend

God is the Judge who forgives and declares you not guilty. Your new state of innocence is not because of anything you have done but only because Christ paid the penalty for you.

God is the Dad who promises to forgive you each and every day, many times a day, when you come to Him in repentance. Your parents may or may not have been forgiving people when you did wrong, but God is the Father who runs to forgive when you come back to Him.

We are the Friend who forgives those who sin against us. This may not be easy to do, but when we recognize the forgiveness we receive from the Judge (for our salvation) and from our Dad (for our daily sins), it is much easier to extend forgiveness to our friends – and even strangers.

Reflection Questions:

1. What are the consequences of not forgiving others?
2. What are the consequences of not asking God to forgive you of your daily sins?
3. Why is it sometimes hard to accept God's forgiveness? What is that saying about God?
4. Who do you need to ask for forgiveness? Who do you need to forgive?
5. How does forgiveness free us from legalism?
6. Why is it an act of self-righteousness to want to add your own works to the cross?
7. Because God is forgiving, I will . . .

"Think-On-It" Verse:

"For if you forgive men when they sin against you, your heavenly Father will also forgive you. But if you do not forgive men their sins, your Father will not forgive your sins."
Matthew 6:14-15

"Before the mountains were born or You
brought forth the earth and the world, from
everlasting to everlasting You are God."
Psalm 90:2

19 - God is Eternal

Practical vs. Theoretical

My all-time least favorite class in college was Introduction to Philosophy 101. I absolutely hated it. I sat there confused the whole semester thinking to myself, "What are all you people talking about? A chair is a chair whether you're sitting in it or not. The chair exists, we exist, that tree over there exists, and not just because we can conceive of them existing. They are! Now let's move on!" This alone was the only thought I ever entertained in that class.

I'm the kind of person who is drawn to the practical things in life. I did not see anything practical in that class. Explaining the benefits of "God is Eternal" could easily become a conversation for any philosophy class. (I think.; like I said, I really had no idea what they were talking about.) But the truth is, we can learn a lot about God's character and nature by looking at this attribute.

Eternal at the Core

The Bible testifies to the fact that God is eternal. It's not just our conjecture or something we figured out about God. But even if the Bible didn't teach us that God is eternal, we would have to infer from His other attributes. If the Biblical writers had no term or word they could use to express absolute everlastingness, we would have to make up a new word to explain the concept because throughout the Bible it is simply assumed, implied, and taken for granted by everyone that God is eternal in His being.[1]

Even though the Bible teaches us that God is eternal, when we look at His other attributes, we would have no choice but to conclude that God is indeed an eternal being.

This attribute of God is much more than just an interesting side note; it plays a major role in who God is. There are serious consequences for us found in the fact that God is eternal, without beginning or end.

The belief in eternity is foundational to the Kingdom of God. In the same way our present world depends on carbon as an essential

126

element to all life, the idea of eternity is needed to give significance and meaning to our Christian doctrine. Our theology largely depends on a God who is eternal and also on the premise that there is an eternity with Him awaiting all those who believe and are saved.[2]

God's eternal nature is at the core of His very essence. If God were not eternal, He would not be God. So everything that God is and everything that God does for us is affected by this eternality. It is foundational to who God is.

What Does God's Eternal Nature Do for Me?
At this point you should be wondering, "How does the fact that God is eternal impact me in any way? I understand that He is eternal; I am not. What does that do for me?" There are some very practical things about God's eternal nature that do have a direct effect on you.

God Sees All Time Equally Vivid
God is infinite; He is eternal, without a beginning or an end. Which means He sees and experiences what we call time very differently than we do.

> "God has no beginning, end, or succession of moments in His own being, and He sees all time equally vivid, yet God sees events in time and acts in time."[3]

Being a finite creature has its limitations. We cannot fly like Superman, we cannot know the number of stars and our bodies will someday stop working. In addition to the "no flying" issue, another downside to our finiteness is that we see time in a linear fashion. To us, there is always a past, present, and a future. We look at life and history on a timeline.

For example, in American history, there is a mark on the timeline when Columbus landed. We move to the right to see another mark when the Declaration of Independence was signed. These marks signify events that happened in the past until they reach us in the present. We can only guess what marks will be placed on the timeline in the future.

God has no timelines to keep track of what has happened in the past. To God everything is happening in His present. We see marks on a timeline in a linear way; He sees these events on a plate. He sees everything all at once.

To Him, at *this very moment* Columbus is discovering America, the American Forefathers are debating the wording of the Declaration of Independence, and man is taking his first steps on the moon.

God Sees All Events in Time and Acts in Time

God is not passively watching these events, unable or unwilling to act or intercede in what we call time.

"But when the time had fully come, God sent His Son born
of a woman, born under law, to redeem those under law."
(Galatians 4:4-5)

God is not just a cosmic observer simply watching the events of our history unfolding before Him. He observes clearly and knows exactly what is happening in His creation. He not only observes; He also daily interacts with His creation. He daily intercedes and orchestrates events, both on a personal level and on a global scale. In the Scriptures we see that when the time was right, "when the time had fully come," He sent Christ into this world to intercede on our behalf and become a sacrifice for us.[4]

Throughout the Scriptures we see clearly where God intervenes and acts in our timeline. In fact, He sovereignly chooses to act differently at different points in time.

"In the past God overlooked such ignorance, but *now* He commands
all people everywhere to repent. *For He has set a day when He will judge
the world* with justice by the man He has appointed. He has given
proof of this to all men by raising Him from the dead."
(Acts 17:30-31)

This verse describes the way God has acted, the way God is acting, and the way God will act in the future. He has a plan to accomplish His will within our history and succession of time.

God is Timeless in His Own Being

From cover to cover, the Word of God tells us that God is Himself eternal. Genesis 1:1 begins with the assumed understanding that before God created all things, He existed. The exodus story of the Hebrew people begins with the proclamation of His name "I AM" in Exodus 3:14.

In Job, Elihu says to his suffering friend, "the number of His years is unsearchable" (Job 36:26). The Psalms repeatedly make this point: "from everlasting to everlasting You are God" (90:2). Finally, Christ Himself testified to this fact in the final book of the Bible when He said,

"I am the Alpha and Omega."
(Revelation 1:8)

I made it through all of my years of schooling without ever taking a physics class, a feat of which I'm quite proud. Evidently, physics tells us that matter and time and space must all occur together. If there is no matter, there can be no space or time either. This means that before God created the universe out of nothing, there was no such thing as time – at least as we see it as a succession of moments one after another.

This means that when God created the universe, time began. God has always existed, even before there was a universe, before there was a succession of moments that we call time. God always existed without ever being influenced by what we call time. Time doesn't have an independent existence in itself, but like the rest of God's creation, it is dependent on His eternal being to mark its existence.[5]

To say that God is timeless in His own being is to say God existed before time began, before there was a succession of moments experienced by His created beings.

Why "God is Eternal" is a BIG DEAL

I *still* may not have answered your questions, "How does the fact that God is eternal impact me?" and "What does God's eternal nature do for me?" Well, your answers are found right here:

Realize that the most painful moments in your past are happening in God's present. At this very moment, God is witnessing the abuse you may have received as a child or the other tragic events that have helped to shape your life. He does not just grieve for your past; He is experiencing the grief of those sins and difficult events in His *right now*.

The cross is not a historical event to God. To us, the crucifixion is an event of long ago in a far off dusty place; but to God, His Son is being spat upon, whipped, and nailed to a cross right now. Christ taking on the sins of the world was not a one-time event. From God's perspective, Christ is being crucified right now. This should affect the way we see our sin, the sacrifice on the cross, and the salvation God makes available to those who believe. It's a big deal.

The temptation that Christ faced while He walked among us is not a distant memory. He is able to sympathize with us when we are tempted because those events of "the past" are happening to Him in the present – right now.

"For we do not have a high priest who cannot sympathize with our weaknesses, but One who has been tempted in all things as we are, yet without sin. Therefore let us draw near with confidence to the throne of grace, so that we may receive mercy and find grace to help in time of need."
(Hebrews 4:15-16)

When we have any need, whether it be saying no to a temptation or something else that is difficult for us to face, God is able to fully sympathize with us in ways we will never fully understand. We must recognize the implications of His eternal nature.

God's sovereignty, wisdom and patience are seen in His eternal nature. Because God sees all events in time as equally vivid, we can trust Him to act wisely in His interactions with us. He sees clearly the results of His actions in our future. God is never surprised. Nothing has ever happened that was unexpected to Him. We can trust His sovereign rule because He sees and experiences the outcome of His every action while performing that very action.

To God, long periods of time are not experienced or felt as they are to us. A thousand years are like a day to Him (Psalm 90:4). We may be tempted to think that God's patience with us is tried and stretched when we continue to struggle with some issue in our lives for extended periods of time. God does not get tired of our failings. He does not view them in the same timeframes that we have imposed upon ourselves.

We benefit from having an eternal mindset. We are far too often focused only on the here and now. Even though we are not eternal, it is to our benefit to consider our actions and how they can have an eternal effect on others. Being oblivious to the eternal leaves us experts in the trivial and novices of the significant. Without an eternal perspective, we tend to major on the momentary and minor on the momentous.

Reflection Questions:

1. What event of your past are you glad God experiences in His present?
2. How is God's patience related to His eternal nature?
3. What would it mean if God were not eternal?
4. How does the temptation of Christ help you with your temptations?
5. What can you do to make a difference for eternity in others?
6. Which Big Deal point do you like best? Why?
7. Because God is eternal, I will . . .

"Think-On-It" Verse:
"The eternal God is your refuge, and
underneath are the everlasting arms."
Deuteronomy 33:27

"You shall not make for yourself an image in the form of anything in heaven above or on the earth beneath or in the waters below. You shall not bow down to them or worship them; for I, the Lord your God, am a jealous God."
Exodus 20:4-5

20 - God is Jealous

The Worst of All Emotions?

Have you ever been jealous? Have you ever had your girlfriend break up with you and then start dating someone else right away? And then everywhere you go, she's there... with *him*. Jealousy is a bad feeling. I've heard.

Jealousy may just be the worst of all the emotions. It's a cocktail of some really ugly feelings all mixed up together. Usually when you're jealous, you're grieving the loss of a relationship. There is pain, anguish, anger, and frustration. Jealousy includes elements of mourning, selfishness, suspicion, and distrust. It leaves you feeling hostile to someone you once held dear. It destroys and leaves you bitter. Jealousy is a bad thing.

God said, "I am a jealous God." Because jealousy is such an unpleasant emotion, many have a difficult time understanding why God would describe Himself in this way.

Envy, Jealousy and Zeal

In Exodus 20:5, the meaning of the word *jealous* is different than in Galatians 5:20 where it's used to describe the sin of jealousy. Envy, jealousy, and zeal are related but convey very different meanings.

Envy is the result of not being content with what God has given you. We are envious when someone has *something* that we desperately want (material possessions or another's ability/skill). Jealousy is the sin of wanting a *relationship* with someone that we do not have. Often we feel jealousy most intensely when someone is in a current relationship with someone we once had a relationship with. A boyfriend can feel jealous when his old girlfriend is dating someone else.

God is not envious of anyone; He already has everything. God is not jealous in that He desires to have a relationship with someone who does not want a relationship with Him. God's jealousy is born out of

His zealous desire for us. He is zealous of protecting those precious to Him, those who belong to Him.

Our jealousy is born out of our unmet needs and insecurity; God's jealousy is the result of His "continually seeking to protect His own honor."[1] He says in the second of the Ten Commandments, "...make no other gods, for I, the Lord your God, am a jealous God" because He is not willing to share His glory with anyone or anything else.

In this commandment, God was referring to His people making idols and worshiping them instead of Him. God is not willing to be shared with anyone. He is possessive of the worship and service that belong only to Him. It is a sin to worship or serve anything other than God.

God can only be jealous for those who are already His. He is never jealous for the unrepentant. He is only jealous for His own children. There is no hint of selfishness or insecurity; it is born out of His holiness and His pure desire for us.

Good and Bad Jealousy
A great example of this godly jealousy is seen in the context of the marriage relationship.

Situation #1 – A husband sees another man speaking innocently with his wife, but he reacts badly because he is insecure or threatened; he assumes the worst. (This type of jealousy would be considered wrong and sinful.)

Situation #2 – A husband sees another man overtly flirting with his wife. He has the right to be jealous because only he has the right to flirt with his wife. (His jealousy is not sinful, because his wife belongs to him.)

Our worship, praise, and affections belong only to God because He is the only one worthy of them. God is perfectly within His rights to be jealous when our devotion is given to anything else. God is zealous of protecting the exclusiveness of our relationship with Him, but even this is for our own good. He knows that when our affections go elsewhere, it is ultimately to our own detriment.

What is at the Core of Your Jealousy?
When we feel jealous, it's because we're thinking of ourselves and what's best for us. Our focus is almost always on *our* wants, *our* hopes, and *our* desires. The truth is, we are always at the center of our jealousy

– not the person you are jealous of. For us, jealousy is always a form of selfishness.

But when God is jealous for us, it's because He's thinking about what's best for us. God's jealousy is not self-serving or born out of His want, unmet needs, or selfish desires; His jealousy is born out of His love and passionate concern for us as His children.

What Would It Say About God If He Were Not Jealous?
It's actually kind of a horrifying thought. You may not like to think of the word *jealousy* being attached to God, but what if He wasn't jealous? What does it say about the husband who doesn't care that another man overtly flirts with his wife at a party? What does it say about how he values their relationship?

Hosea was an Old Testament prophet who was told by God to marry someone who was unfaithful to him. It was a painful object lesson for the Hebrew people to see their unfaithfulness to God lived out before their very eyes. If God were not jealous, He would have no problem with us running around and "cheating" on Him. Fortunately, God does have a big problem when our affections are drawn elsewhere!

Why "God is Jealous" is a BIG DEAL
That God "continually seeks to protect His honor" says something about how He sees Himself. He does not see Himself as merely a good option out of the many you consider; He sees Himself as the *only* option. God says He is the only thing you need in this life because He is the best thing in this life. If God did not think so highly of Himself, He would not be worthy of our worship, praise, adoration, and affection.

Not only does God seek to protect His *honor*. He seeks to protect His *own*. God knows that the best thing for us is Him. He knows that when we worship anything else, we are settling for infinitely less than the best. Out of both pity and concern for our well-being He is jealous for us.

He desires for us to live lives that are full, rich, meaningful, and glorifying to Him. He is jealous when we settle for far less than the best found in Him. C.S. Lewis expressed it well:
> "We are half-hearted creatures, fooling about with drink and sex
> and ambition when infinite joy is offered us, like an ignorant child
> who wants to go on making mud pies in a slum because he cannot

imagine what is meant by the offer of a holiday at the sea. We are far too easily pleased."[2]

God is both jealous and zealous for us because we are His chosen ones. In the Old Testament, God viewed the Hebrew people as His special possession, set aside for His purposes. In the New Testament, we as believers are depicted as His bride.

Everyone has a specialness about them because we are all are created in His image, but for those who believe in Him, He has a special desire and feeling of ownership. He is jealous because we are His and He is ours. He is a consuming fire who is jealous for the purity of the covenant relationship He has with us.

Because God is jealous, we must kill our idols of the heart. The heart is an idol factory. It does not carve idols out of wood or stone; it is much more clever and devious than that. No, the heart creates idols out of good things. An idol of the heart is anything we have in our lives that we depend on more than God. When a good thing becomes a god thing, it's a bad thing. An idol of the heart can be defined this way:

> "It is anything more important to you than God, anything that absorbs your heart and imagination more than God, anything you seek to give you what only God can give."[3]

What is the "anything you seek to give you what only God can give" in your life? We are needy creatures full of wants and desires. Our hearts continually search for that something or that someone who will bring us lasting peace, reassurance, and contentment.

Christians may say that someone is God. We may sincerely believe that our relationship with Him *is* that something we depend on for fulfillment and joy, but chances are, if we look a bit deeper, there are other things in our lives on which we find ourselves depending for a measure of happiness, security, and contentment. These things can easily become our idols of the heart – and they inflame the jealousy of God.

They can include a list of very good things: your spouse, your kids, your job, your abilities, and even your ministry opportunities. But the truth is, if you depend on any of these things to give you what only God can give, you may have an idol issue. Even these good things may be attempting to fill a role that only God can satisfy.

We all may have to ask on occasion, "How do I inflame the jealousy of God?" We all need to look at our lives and consider what idols of the heart we may have. What are the things in your life that satisfy your desires? In what things are you finding your security?

God is not content to be one of the things that helps get you through this life. He wants your whole heart – not just a part. He knows that we cannot serve two masters, and He refuses to be shared with another – even if the "another" is a good thing – because it will never be the best thing for us.

Ultimately, our idols always interfere in our relationship with God.

"Then the word of the Lord came to me: 'Son of man, these
men have set up idols in their hearts and put wicked stumbling
blocks before their faces. Should I let them inquire of me at all?'"
(Ezekiel 14:2-3)

Reflection Questions:

1. When was a time that you were jealous?
2. Why were you jealous? Were you truly concerned for the other person or for yourself?
3. Explain what God would be like if He were not jealous.
4. Do you see any examples of godly jealousy in the life of Christ?
5. Do you have any idols of the heart? What are they?
6. Why does God continually seek to protect His own honor? Why is God so zealous for us?
7. Because God is jealous, I will . . .

"Think-On-It" Verse:

"You shall not bow down to them or worship them;
for I, the Lord your God, am a jealous God, punishing
the children for the sin of the fathers to the third and
fourth generation of those who hate Me."
Deuteronomy 5:9

"Your attitude should be the same as that of Christ Jesus:
Who, being in very nature God, did not consider equality
with God something to be grasped, but made Himself nothing,
taking the very nature of a servant, being made in human likeness. And being found in appearance as a man, He humbled
Himself and became obedient to death – even death on a cross!"
Philippians 2:5-8

21 - God is Humble

"O Divine Spirit, who efface Yourself before the Father and Son;
O Jesus, meek and humble of heart; O Abba Father,
who humble Yourself to commune with the lowly;
O beautiful Trinity, You are Humility!"
- Saint Francis of Assisi, *The Praises of God*

What Kind of Crazy Talk is This?

God is humble. That is a sentence you most likely have never read before. In fact, this is a concept you probably have some serious doubts about. You may be more than wondering about it; you may be contemplating skipping this attribute altogether for another one more sensible.

After all, you just read about God's jealousy due to the fact that He is the Almighty God who refuses to share His glory with anyone. If God cannot stand for our affections being placed anywhere else, how can we say with our very next breath that He is also humble?

When you think of God, you think of power and majesty, fear and trembling. You think of the Supreme Being who created everything, can do anything, and sustains the universe (*His* universe) moment by moment. How can the word *humility* be attached to the unapproachable light? To most, assigning the attribute of humility to the Most High is more than strange; it almost seems a bit inappropriate.

Saint Francis of Assisi thought humility was one of God's attributes, and he knew a lot more about God than I do. So it's worth asking: "Is God humble?"

What is Humility?

Let's start with the question, "What is humility?" If we have a wrong understanding of that, we will draw the wrong conclusions about God's humility.

Humility is not walking around all day feeling that you are inferior to everyone else. Entertaining thoughts that you are worse than or less than you really are is not living out the virtue of humility. Humility is having a proper and balanced understanding of yourself. It is the total absence of conceit, haughtiness, and arrogance.

God has a proper understanding of Himself. He knows Himself better than we know ourselves. If anyone has no illusions about Himself, it's God. If this is true, then God could never be accused of being arrogant or prideful because pride is the sin of thinking you're better than you really are.

He is What He Thinks He Is
God is the Supreme Being, which means He can never think more highly of Himself than He really is. God understands and comprehends Himself perfectly, so He is not arrogant, puffed up, or ostentatious in His opinion of Himself. He is what He thinks He is. That's not pride; that's reality.

God does not have a problem with saying who He is. God does demand worship and adoration from us, this is true. But this demand is not born out of His arrogance or insecurity; it comes from the simple fact that God truly *deserves* our worship. It is not an act of longing ego to demand what you rightfully deserve.

If your next door neighbor demanded your worship and adoration, that would be the result of their conceit, arrogance, or plain stupidity because they obviously have done nothing to deserve it. But when you are *THE* transcendent being of the universe, which is infinitely greater than everything you have created, you then have the right to demand praise from your creation.

God Never Chases Anyone
Here's a thought to ponder: God never chases anyone. He may run to forgive, but He never chases anyone in that He is desperate or wanting of someone to want Him. He does call out to us; He does reveal Himself; He does desire for all men to know Him; He may even pursue us; but He never chases us in desperation.

In humility God says, "I am the Almighty God. You need to recognize that and worship Me, but if you choose to reject Me, I will not chase you down and beg for you to reconsider your decision."

This can be seen in Romans 1 where God not only refuses to chase those who follow darkness, He does the exact opposite; He hands them over to the wickedness they have chosen. Three times in this one chapter God says He "gave them over" – first, to the "sinful desires of their hearts" (vs.24), then to "shameful lusts" (vs. 26), and finally to a "depraved mind" (vs. 28).

Humility and Self-Sufficiency

God's humility is tied to His self-sufficiency. He does not need us, but He does desire for us to have a relationship with Him. He may want it. He may even long for it. He died for it. But He does not need it, and He is willing to let you reject Him because He is also a humble God.

The Scriptures and the Humility of God

The Scriptures give evidence and testify to this attribute of humility in each member of the Trinity.

The Humility of Jesus

The Apostle Paul tells us that Jesus,

> "made Himself nothing, taking the very nature of
> a servant, being made in human likeness. And being
> found in appearance as a man, He humbled Himself and
> became obedient to death – even death on a cross!"
> (Philippians 2:7-8)

Jesus spoke of His own humility when He said,

> "Take my yoke upon you and learn from Me, for I am gentle
> and humble in heart, and you will find rest for your souls."
> (Matthew 11:29)

What is the heart of Jesus? This is not a difficult question to answer. In Matthew 11:28-29, Christ told us plainly that He is "gentle and *humble* in heart." The heart of Jesus stands radically opposed to the principles promoted by the world. It identifies closely with the plight of the weak and disenfranchised. It is a heart that compels Him to wash the feet of others and lay down His life for His friends.

In doing these things, Jesus not only became our example, He also revealed to us the deepest concerns of His Father in heaven (John

14:9). Since Christ's humility is at the core of His being, and since He is the revelation of the Godhead, it is reasonable to infer that the Father and the Spirit must also share this attribute of humility.

The Humility of the Holy Spirit

Humility is also seen in the continuing ministry of the Holy Spirit. Jesus said of the One that would follow Him, "He will bring glory to Me by taking from what is Mine and making it known to you" (John 16:14). Here, Jesus is telling us that the Holy Spirit, while still a member of the triune Godhead, chooses only to glorify Christ, not Himself.

The Humility of the Father

But what about the Father? Jesus submits to the Father in His taking on flesh, and the Spirit submits to the Father and Son in His continuing ministry to the Body. Does the Father display humility to anyone in the Scriptures?

The Father's humility is seen in His desire for fellowship with us.

> "Who is like the Lord our God, Who is enthroned
> on high, who humbles Himself to behold the
> things that are in heaven and in the earth?"
> (Psalm 113:5-6 NASB)

The Father shows a measure of humility in two ways. First, He desires to have fellowship with the fallen and sinful creatures that we are. We are depraved and unworthy of His affections due to our sin, yet He desires for us to be called His own. Our adoption into His family as sons and daughters is an indication of His humility.

Secondly, God loves the humble and contrite. Conversely, He hates the proud and the haughty. The Father embraces humility by ignoring human grandeur and what we consider of great importance by choosing to associate with the lowly. God not only loves sinners, He loves the worst of all sinners and the least of all people. God's value of humility is seen continually in the scriptures.

> "Though the Lord is on high, He looks upon the
> lowly, but the proud He knows from afar."
> (Psalm 138:6)

> "This is the one I esteem: he who is humble and
> contrite in spirit, and trembles at My word."
> (Isaiah 66:2)

"For thus says the high and lofty One who inhabits eternity, whose name is Holy: 'I dwell in the high and holy place, and also with him who is of a contrite and humble spirit, to revive the spirit of the humble, and to revive the heart of the contrite.'"
(Isaiah 57:15)

Other Evidences of the Humility of God

Humility in Birth

God's value of humility can also be seen in God's choice of the Savior's birthplace and birth parents. Unwed teens were told they were to be parents of the Most High. Jesus was born to a poor family in a poor country suffering under Roman occupation.

A pregnant Mary rejoiced that God had chosen her, a humble servant, to bless all the generations (Luke 1:48) and that the mighty deeds of God include lifting up the humble and scattering the proud (1:51-52). God values humility so much that He chose for His Son to enter the world through humble parents of humble means.

Humility in Love

God is a loving God (1 John 4:8). The word used for *love* here is *agape*. Agape is a self-sacrificial love. God loves us with this type of agape love. Paul tells us that this kind of love "is not proud. It is not rude, it is not self-seeking" (1 Corinthians 13:4-5).

Agape love, God's love for us, is not proud or self-serving; it is sacrificial in nature. This type of sacrificial love for fallen humanity requires a God with humility as part of His character.

Humility in Death

The humility of God is also seen in His sacrifice at the cross. In the movie *The Passion of the Christ,* great care was taken to make sure the gospel accounts were followed as closely as possible. It was a violent movie. It was an R-rated picture due to the graphic nature of Christ's crucifixion. The beatings, the blood, and the brutality were difficult to watch.

There was one thing, however, that the filmmaker did do to make it easier on the viewer – they put some clothes on Jesus. Every painting and crucifix you see will have Jesus in a loin cloth, but the reality is that Jesus humbled Himself on the cross in ways we do not want to imagine.

141

The humility of God is also seen in the very plan of salvation. God values humility and weakness so much so that He chose the humiliating death of the cross to save the proud and the arrogant.

"God chose the weak things of the world to shame the strong.
He chose the lowly things of this world and the despised things
and the things that are not – to nullify the things that are."
(1 Corinthians 1:23, 27-28)

The cross is seen as complete and utter foolishness to men, but it is the ultimate wisdom of God. It runs contrary to our way of thinking. We think the strong, confident, and proud are the only ones who can accomplish great things in this life, but God used the naked humiliation of the cross to save a world that mocked, beat, and spat upon the sacrifice for our sins.

Why "God is Humble" is a BIG DEAL

It fights a "wrong thought" about God. Most people reject God because they make many wrong assumptions about Him. Millions of people think of God as arrogant. They find the claim of Christ that "I am the way, and the truth, and the life; no one comes to the Father but through Me" (John 14:6) the height of this arrogance. But correct thinking about God acknowledges His humility.

When you recognize that humility is also an attribute of God, you then have a fuller picture of all He is. God is not proud, but He never backs down from who He is. He stands by each and every claim He makes about Himself.

It's a relationship. Relationships are based on choice. Unless you are in a pre-arranged marriage, you chose your spouse, and they chose you. God is humble enough to never force Himself upon you. He is humble enough to let you walk away if that is your desire. He will never chase you down to beg for your allegiance.

A life to imitate. Our desire to imitate Christ obviously challenges us to live a life of humility with the same sort of self-sacrificial love that God has for us. You may never walk on water, heal the lame, give sight to the blind, or turn water into wine (which is most unfortunate), but you can be Christlike by living a life marked by humility.

Jesus once healed a blind man by spitting into the dirt to make mud for his eyes. How many times did He have to spit to make enough mud? Spitting to make mud was a humbling thing to do. His making "spit-mud" also shows that Christ was not afraid to get dirty with us. He humbled Himself to get into our complicated messes. We should be willing to do the same with those around us who need our help.

The hurt of humiliation. Sometimes humility is a choice when we choose to humble ourselves by serving others or putting their needs before our own, but on occasion humility is forced upon us; at times it hits us like a sledgehammer. We call this humiliation, and it usually hurts a lot.

During these painful times, you are possibly the most like Christ that you will ever be. Christ knows the pain of not being appreciated. He knows the experience of rejection. He knows how you feel. God uses these humbling times to conform you into the image of His Son. As harsh as it may sound, God will break your bones to get your heart.

Future ministry. We are better able to help others after we have had hurtful or humiliating experiences. God can use these experiences to allow you to minister to others who are humbled in painful ways. They make us more sensitive to the needs of others (2 Corinthians 1:3-4).

Humility also brings submission, and submission ushers in the anointing of God to whatever we put our hand. This is because true humility and submission will always lead us to the realization that it is truly God who is working through us and that we can in fact take no credit for the things that He may accomplish through our efforts.

Humility kills pride. Few think themselves arrogant, but we all have issues of pride. Our pride gets in the way of living lives that imitate His, mostly in ways we are never aware. Godly people walk with a limp because, like Jacob, they have met God and they are fully aware of their own weakness and need. Our pride takes many forms, but always has one goal: our own self-glorification.

Pride runs contrary to the gospel and to understanding what grace is all about. Pride says I did this. It unwittingly pushes God out of the picture.

> "When we find pride in the church, we can be sure there are
> believers there who don't really understand the gospel. Pride can
> never exist where the gospel is clearly understood."[1]

If we're not careful, we may start thinking that our righteousness is actually the result of our effort and not Christ's work on the cross. We'll start to think our good works, our obedience, and our efforts to live righteous lives actually give us a righteous standing before God. True humility kills this pride and helps us to realize the futility of such self-righteous behavior.

Humility protects us. Jonathan Edwards once wrote, "Nothing sets a person so much out of the devil's reach as humility."[2] Our humility keeps us recognizing our continual need for God, and that our lives are truly dependent on Him. This attitude is always good for us in the long run.

Humility draws us closer to Him. God loves the contrite. His blessings are promised to the humble; none are promised to the proud. God loves the humility of our honesty. He learns nothing new when we are humble and transparent before Him, but we can learn nothing new about Him without humility.

We actually undermine our own prayers when we pray to be Christlike and then go on living our lives following our own hopes, dreams, and aspirations instead of humbly seeking His will.

Humility alone allows for true confession and true repentance, and no one can draw near to God without confessing and repenting of all the wrong they have done and continue to do each day. Humility ushers in the grace of God that we all so desperately need to experience in our lives.

Reflection Questions:

1. What is your objection to the idea that God is humble?
2. How would you describe humility and pride?
3. What aspects of God's humility do you appreciate the most?
4. How would you describe God's humility to an unsaved friend or family member?
5. How is pride seen in your life?
6. Why are you hesitant to serve others with more humility?
7. Because God is humble, I will . . .

"Think-On-It" Verse:
"God resists the proud but
gives grace to the humble."
1 Peter 5:5

"A man had a fig tree, planted in his vineyard, and he went to look for fruit on it, but did not find any. So he said to the man who took care of the vineyard, 'For three years now I've been coming to look for fruit on this fig tree and haven't found any. Cut it down! Why should it use up the soil?' "'Sir,' the man replied, 'leave it alone for one more year, and I'll dig around it and fertilize it. If it bears fruit next year, fine! If not, then cut it down.'"

Luke 13:6-8

22 - God is Patient

Patience and Parenting

A few weeks after our first child was born, someone asked me if being a parent had changed me at all. Without even thinking I replied, "I wash my hands a lot more now." If you've ever changed a diaper, you understand the significance of that answer.

Being a parent brings many changes into your life. Besides the continual hand washing when they're infants and the hand wringing when they're teens, raising kids stretches you in the area of patience like no other experience ever will.

God's Patience Was First Seen in the Garden

God is patient. We see this played out in the first few pages of the Bible. When His children did the very *one thing* that He instructed them *not* to do in the garden paradise, He exhibited patience. For many of us, our first reaction would have been to scream out in anger, "You did what!?"

How did God react? His reaction to their sin was marked by patience. He talked calmly and asked them what they had done in a seemingly measured tone. It's been mentioned in the discussion of other attributes, and it will be mentioned again here, that God shows both patience and mercy with the immediate promise to send Another (Jesus) who will one day crush the head of Satan, the deceiving serpent (Genesis 3:15).

There were consequences to their sin, to be sure; we still suffer those consequences today. But Adam and Eve were not crushed, they were not "smote," they were not disowned and banished from a relationship with God. They were allowed to have children and live long lives.

Patience in the Old Testament

God is patient and longsuffering. This example in the garden is only the first of many. Throughout the scriptures it is easy to see that God delays and defers judgment on a people who are deserving of His anger, wrath, and immediate justice. Throughout the Bible narrative, "God is pictured as withholding judgment and continuing to offer salvation and grace over long periods of time."[1]

The best example of God's patience that we can relate to is His dealing with His chosen Hebrew people.

"God's long-suffering was particularly apparent with Israel; this was, of course, an outflow of His faithfulness to them. The people of Israel repeatedly rebelled against Jehovah, desiring to return to Egypt, rejecting Moses' leadership, setting up idols for worship, falling into the practices of the people about them, and intermarrying with them. A large scale destruction of Israel on the fashion of the flood would have been appropriate, yet the Lord did not cut them off."[2]

When we read of the continuing folly of the Hebrew people 3,500 years ago, we can easily recognize the patience of God. Of course, there were times when His patience was tried and tested, but He continually chose to withhold His anger from them. There were consequences to be suffered, but there were also continual blessings to be had by a people who deserved judgment instead of the patience and mercy they continually received.

Patience in the New Testament

The patience of God is exhibited in the New Testament as well, specifically in two different ways. First, the life of Christ was marked by patience. Examine His life closely, and you will see time and again that He dealt most patiently with the lost and with those who had little or no spiritual understanding. Oddly enough, the people Jesus did not have much patience with were the religious establishment of the day. His interactions with the Pharisees and Sadducees and His turning over of the tables in the temple court show us that He was far less patient with those who knew better; than He was with those who lived in spiritual darkness.

Secondly, the patience of God is seen in the current delaying of punishment and judgment of the world.

"The Lord is not slow in keeping His promise, as
some understand slowness. He is patient with you,
not wanting anyone to perish, but everyone to come to

repentance…Bear in mind that our Lord's patience
means salvation, just as our dear brother Paul also
wrote you with the wisdom that God gave him."
(2 Peter 3:9, 15)

We are all currently experiencing God's patience each and every day. It seems that He is withholding His judgment out of His desire to see more of us come to a saving knowledge and faith in Him.

The Power of Patience

Some may wonder at this point, "Is God's patience a power unto itself, or is it the result of His power of righteousness not being released upon creation?" "Is God actively exercising restraint on the evil that He sees each day, or is He passively waiting to act upon the rebellion that is unfolding before Him?"

Arthur Pink argued that God is actively exercising a power of restraint, His power of patience.

"The patience of God is that Excellency which causes Him to
sustain great injuries without immediately avenging Himself. He
has a power of patience as well as a power of justice."[3]

Note that God's patience is active even though our sin is injurious to Him. We most often fail to recognize God's hatred for sin. He finds it an offense against him, not just a trapping of pleasure into which we fall. Sin is a big deal because God says it's a big deal.

There is a power of patience that is an active attribute of God. His patience is not just the absence of His acting upon evil. Moses testified to this when he interceded on behalf of the rebellious Hebrew people:

"Now may the Lord's strength be displayed, just
as you have declared: 'The Lord is slow to anger,
abounding in love and forgiving sin and rebellion.'"
(Numbers 14:17)

Here God showed His power and strength by *not* giving the nation of Israel what they deserved. "His long suffering is His power of self-restraint."[4]

Patience and Justice

Obviously God's patience is closely tied with His love, mercy, and goodness, but it is also balanced by His justice and righteousness. Unforgiven sin will never go unpunished, but God's patience allows time for repentance. This time allowed for repentance also applies to

147

those who once proclaimed Christ as Savior but then live a life inconsistent with that truth.

Christians will always sin, but the life of a disciple should never be marked by continual and unrepentant sin. God's patience is seen in His withholding of judgment on the non-believer, but it is also seen in His forbearance with those who once proclaimed Christ but then failed to pursue living lives in accordance with that decision.

Patience Abused

We must also realize the sad truth that God's patience is something that the unbelieving world takes advantage of and abuses.

> "When the sentence for a crime is not quickly carried out, the hearts of the people are filled with schemes to do wrong."
> (Ecclesiastes 8:11)

The Christian sees God's patience as an act of mercy and further proof of His goodness, but the unbeliever sees it as a license, an excuse, to do more wrong.[5] God is patient with us when we sin; He is not lenient. It's vitally important that we never confuse the two.

God's Patience and His Eternal Nature

Because He sees all events in time equally vivid, God views the passage of time differently than we do. To God, long periods of time are not experienced or felt as they are to us. A thousand years are like a day to Him (Psalm 90:4).

We may be tempted to think that God's patience with us is tried and stretched when we struggle for extended periods of time. God does not get tired of our failings. He does not view them with the same time frames that we have imposed upon ourselves.

Sovereign Patience

God is patient because He always knows what you are going to do ahead of time. God is patient because He already covered the cost of all your moral failures at the cross. God is patient because He realizes that you can do nothing of value without His help. To those who know and walk with God, His patience is something we do not fully realize or appreciate.

Again, God's sovereignty has already accounted for your failures. Jerry Bridges wrote:

> "Does failure on our part to act prudently frustrate the sovereign plan of God? The scriptures never indicate that God is frustrated

148

to any degree by our failure to act as we should. In His infinite wisdom, God's sovereign plan includes our failures and even our sins."[6]

Why "God is Patient" is a BIG DEAL

His patience is something to ponder and appreciate. The patience of God is not talked about as much as His mercy and His grace, but it is something we are to deeply admire and appreciate. We are all recipients of God's patience in one form or another every day. God is more patient with us than we realize. We can always appeal to Him for whatever we need (Psalm 86:16; Zechariah 1:12).

God is patient to forgive. We often fail to fully recognize God's forgiveness when we sin because we never fully understand how patient God is with us. He is long-suffering with us and our struggles. It is a lie of Satan's too easily believed that God will not forgive us because His patience has run out.

We are to imitate God's patience. Because we are on the receiving end of God's patience, we are to be givers of patience to others also. Jesus told his disciples to forgive an offense 490 times. This type of countless and continual forgiveness cannot happen without patience and godly love for others.

We are to be "slow to anger" (James 1:9), "patient in suffering" (1 Peter 2:20), "humble and gentle, patient, bearing with one another in love" (Ephesians 4:2). This sort of Biblical patience is not easy for us; in fact, it may just be impossible when attempted under our own power.

Like the other attributes that we are told to imitate, showing patience requires trusting in God to fulfill His promises and His purposes according to His timing, not ours. When we believe that God will accomplish His goals for our good and His glory, it is much easier to be patient.[7]

In fact, patience is one of the Fruits of the Spirit listed in Galatians 5:22: love, joy, peace, patience, kindness, goodness, faithfulness, gentleness, and self-control. It's not a quality that we can opt out of if we so desire.

We are to be patient with God's timing. Because God is patient with us, we can be patient with His timing for the things we desire to see happen in our lives. In many respects, everything we do indicates

149

our beliefs about God. When we're not patient for His timing, we buy things we cannot afford, we cross sexual boundaries in dating relationships, we may even marry someone who's not a great fit for us. When we're not patient, we jump ahead and take the reins in an attempt to take control. A lack of patience often indicates a belief within us that God will not meet our wants and needs.

We are a culture that demands immediate gratification. We don't like to wait for anything. Some of us grow impatient when it takes 60 seconds to microwave a burrito. But God is patient with us and our growth. We need to show this same kind of patience with Him and His sovereign timing for our lives.

Patience brings wisdom and direction to our lives. When we learn to be patient with God's timing, we grow in our wisdom and understanding. Patience plays an essential role in discerning God's will. The Bible is full of examples of those who acted foolishly because they were not willing to wait patiently for God's direction.

> "But they soon forgot what He had
> done and did not wait for His counsel."
> (Psalm 106:13)

God's silence is not always a bad thing because it increases our dependence on Him. In fact, there may be no way to discern God's will in our lives without a measure of patience and of waiting on Him to speak. As we wait, our own selfish desires may be tested and quenched for our own good. God must be sought and we must be willing to wait patiently for Him to answer.

Patience shows that we trust God and His sovereignty. The Old Testament stories of King David are fascinating, but the stories of his life before he was king are also incredibly compelling. There are many lessons we can learn by looking at his life. There are many characteristics to emulate and some to avoid.

In many respects, you can argue that David showed an amazing amount of patience with God's timing. He knew that he would one day be King of Israel, but he never forced the issue. Once while he was alone in a cave with King Saul (who, by the way, was trying to kill David), he passed up his chance to take the king's life and claim the throne for his own (1 Samuel 24).

David was willing to wait on God's timing because he trusted God. He knew that he would one day become King, but he was willing to let

God sovereignly bring that day about. He did not feel the need to assert himself, protect his rights, or ensure that that promise would come to pass. He trusted God to bring it about in His time and by His means.

Showing patience is evidence that we are pursuing God in relationship. David also wrote about waiting on God for deliverance and peace. When we wait on God for anything, we prove to Him our desire to walk in relationship with Him – not just have a belief in Him.

> "I waited patiently for the Lord; He turned to me and heard my cry. He lifted me out of the slimy pit, out of the mud and mire; He set my feet on a rock and gave me a firm place to stand."
> (Psalm 40:1-2)

Many people have walked away from their faith because they did not have the patience God may have been asking from them. God desires relationship – not just belief. And belief can easily crumble for many when God does not give them what they want, when they want it. All worthwhile relationships require a measure of persistence, perseverance, and patience.

Reflection Questions:

1. Why does the world often assume God is not patient?
2. How would you have reacted to Adam and Eve's sin?
3. What are some examples of Christ's patience? of His impatience?
4. What does it say about God's character that His patience is a power unto itself?
5. Do you think you can disappoint God? Why or why not? (See the Extra Stuff Appendix)
6. What are you waiting patiently for God to do?
7. Because God is patient, I will . . .

"Think-On-It" Verse:

"Therefore, as God's chosen people, holy and dearly loved, clothe yourselves with compassion, kindness, humility, gentleness and patience."
Colossians 3:12

"I am the way and the truth and the life. No
one comes to the Father except through Me."
John 14:6

23 - God is Truth

Sidewalk, Sunday School and Seminary Answers

Why did Jesus come to earth? When asked this question, your answer
may fall into one of three categories: sidewalk answers, Sunday school
answers, or seminary answers.

Sidewalk answers are those from average people you would meet on
the sidewalk – those without much of a church background or spiritual
knowledge. Sunday school answers are the ones a few of us may have
learned from going to church. Seminary answers are the in-depth,
thoughtful answers with big, confusing words.

Sidewalk answers might include that He came to be a good example or
moral teacher. Jewish people would admit He was a rabbi. Muslims
would say He was a prophet of Allah. Others might even answer that
He's the Son of God or that He came to die for our sins, but chances
are, they really don't understand the significance of their own answers.

Sunday school answers would be along the lines of that He came to be
a sacrifice for our sins or to give us eternal life when we accept Him as
our Lord and Savior. These are obviously the right answers, but not
the best and most complete answers.

Seminary answers might sound something like this: "The incarnational
ministry of Christ and His atoning death on the cross is either
substitutionary, satisfactory, recapitulative, redemptive, reconciliatory,
or propitiationary depending on your own theological premises or
outlook."

Jesus Came to Testify to the Truth

The most accurate way to answer the question, Why did Jesus come to
earth, might simply be this: Jesus came to testify to the truth. This
reply may be the most complete one because it encompasses much
more than just the issue of salvation. In no way do I wish to diminish
the work of Christ on the cross or the power of the resurrection, but
Jesus came to be more than just an atoning sacrifice for our sins; He
came to testify to God's truth in three meaningful ways.

First, Jesus came to testify to and make known a truth that provides a moral standard of living and an expectation of a holy lifestyle. (Jesus gave instruction on how we are to love one another and live our lives for God's glory).

Second, God's truth stands opposed to the lies of Satan and the human worldview. (Jesus provides an alternative way that is in direct opposition to our fleshly desires and normal practice in an unbelieving world).

Third, it confirms both the Old Testament truths and authenticates the future truth of the New Testament not yet realized. Jesus often quoted and endorsed the truth of the Old Testament. He also validated truth that had not yet occurred (We often forget that Jesus' last recorded words are found in the Book of Revelation).

Jesus had more than one mission during His time on earth. He came to demonstrate, teach, and verify the truthfulness of God. He came to do more than just die and rise again. God's desire for us to know His truth was so important to Him that He came in the person of Christ to tell us Himself.

When we say "God is truth," what do we really mean? In the same manner that God is the very standard of holiness and goodness, He is also the final standard of truth. He is the only true God in that all His knowledge and all His words are both true and the final standard of what is true.[1] This short definition has three very important elements to it that need to be more fully explained.

Three Truths of God

First, Jesus testified that His father is the only true God (John 17:3). Back then, His teaching stood in opposition to a culture that worshipped many competing gods. Today, His teaching stands opposed to a culture that is content to have many different gods happily co-existing together. Our pluralistic society denies the existence of only one God. All it asks of you is to be somewhat sincere in whatever faith best fits you.

Second, when we recognize that all His knowledge and words are true, we again see God's multiple attributes working together. When God's knowledge and words are always true, it's because He is the omniscient, all-knowing God. To believe that God knows everything is to say that He is never mistaken in His understanding of the world. In fact, He alone has the only correct understanding of reality.[2]

153

Because God is omniscient, He can never mislead or be untruthful, either intentionally or accidentally. He cannot knowingly or unknowingly tell a lie. He has no choice in the matter; God can only be truthful with us.

> "God represents things as they really are. Whether He is speaking of Himself or part of His creation, what God says is the way things really are."[3]

Third, not only is God the only one who is always true in words and knowledge, but He is the final standard of what is truth. Earlier the point was made that God is not love, but that He is loving. (Love is a *description* of God, not a *definition*). That same argument cannot be made here: God is both truthful *and* truth itself. As God is the very standard of holiness, He is also the standard of truth. God is truth because God is holy, and His truthfulness to us is a result of His holiness.

In a world that has no consensus on what is truth, it's vitally important that we realize what truth is and from where it comes. Truth cannot simply be what most people agree on; it must have an objective standard. God's words are not true because they conform to a standard of truthfulness outside of God. They are truth itself. They are the lasting standard and definition of truth. This is why Jesus can say to the Father, "Your word is truth" in John 17:17.[4]

Using God's holiness as an example, whatever is like God is holy; what is not like God is sin. If this is correct, then whatever is like God is true, and whatever is not like God is false. In essence, whatever conforms to God's Word is true; what fails to conform to His Word is not true.[5]

Why "God is Truth" is a BIG DEAL

Truth and Salvation: Is this only a theological or philosophical discussion with little or no practical value? Your thoughts might be a bit confused on what all this means. But what we all must remember is this: when Christ says, "I am the way, the truth and the life" (John 14:6), He is telling all who will listen that He is the only way to the Father.

Truth and Circumstances: When Pilate had his audience with Christ, he asked, "What is truth?" Today he might have asked, "What is truth to you?" For many, truth is largely whatever we decide it is. It's whatever we feel most comfortable with or whatever will not offend someone else. When Christ said, "I am the truth," He was saying something basic and foundational to those who would follow Him, but also something that was complete and utter nonsense to those who do not believe.

The problem is obvious: when truth is something we determine, it is not a solid foundation; it is a house built on sand. It shifts, moves, and changes. It is built on nothing more than our circumstances or our present desires. When our desires change, then our truth changes. When our circumstances are good, we believe the truth of God's goodness, but when things go bad, for many this truth of His goodness, faithfulness, and wisdom is doubted and in question.

Truth and Postmodernism: Postmodern thought tells us there's no such thing as absolute truth; no such thing as meaning; no such thing as certainty. Once while lecturing at Ohio State University, Ravi Zacharias was shown a new building on campus called the Wexner Center. He was told by his host that it was America's first post-modern building. In an address to the United Nations Prayer Breakfast, Ravi shared the foolishness seen in the thought of both a postmodern building and mindset.

> "I was startled for a moment and I said, 'What is a postmodern building?' He said, 'Well, the architect said that he designed this building with no design in mind.' When the architect was asked why, he said, 'If life itself is capricious, why should our buildings have any design and any meaning?' 'So he has pillars that have no purpose. He has stairways that go nowhere. He has a senseless building built and somebody has paid for it.' I said, 'So his argument was that if life has no purpose and design, why should the building have any design?' He said, 'That is correct.' I said, 'Did he do the same with the foundation?' All of a sudden there was silence. You see, you and I can fool with the infrastructure as much as we would like, but we dare not fool with the foundation because it will call our bluff in a hurry."[6]

There is a foundational truth that holds everything else up and everything all together. This truth is revealed to us in the Scriptures, not decided upon by a majority or popular current trends.

Truth and Integrity: If God is always truthful, so should we be imitators of Him in our interaction with others. We are to be a people of integrity in all we say, all we do, and even in what we may imply. We are to live lives markedly different than those around us. While stretching the truth or cutting corners may be seen as the norm and acceptable to most, it should not be the norm or acceptable to us.

God told His chosen people,

> "Do not have two differing weights in your bag – one heavy, one light.
> Do not have two differing measures in your house – one large, one
> small. You must have accurate and honest weights and measures, so
> that you may live long in the land the Lord your God is giving you."
> (Deuteronomy 25:13-51)

God loves truth, and conversely He hates falsehood (Proverbs 12:22).

Truth and Image Bearers: Why does God hate lying and deceit?
What's wrong with a little white lie? Why is being truthful so incredibly
important to Him? The answer goes beyond the normal understanding
that great harm and trouble can come as a result.

God hates lying for a much deeper and more profound reason. It's
because when we lie, we diminish His glory. We are created in His
image, and when image bearers lie or act deceitfully, we do the exact
opposite of what He planned for us. His desire is for us to reflect His
glory, not to do the opposite. We are acting contrary to God's own
character when we lie or act without integrity.[7]

Being an image bearer of God is a great honor; it's what sets us apart
from everything else that has been created. But it also comes with
great responsibility. Image bearers of God should always reflect the
truth of God. We dishonor and diminish the glory of God when we lie
because we are created to reflect His glory. That's why lying is such a
serious issue: instead of reflecting His glory – we are doing the exact
opposite.

Truth and Relationship: When we seek God's truth, we are not
simply looking for information; we are wanting to know what God is
really like. We want to know *Him* – and not just more *about* Him.

When we finally understand that God is the source of all truth, we
then look to Him for guidance in all things. But, we should never be
satisfied with only knowing what is truth; we need to see His truth in
action – and experience first hand in a relationship with Him.

Reflection Questions:

1. What would your first answer be to, "Why did Jesus come to earth?"
2. Without looking over the chapter, to what truths did Christ come to testify?
3. Why is objective truth rejected and seen as foolishness by so many today?
4. How would you define postmodernism? How would you answer it?
5. Is your truth based on God's Word or your circumstances?
6. How can you better reflect God's truth with your life?
7. Because God is truth, I will . . .

"Think-On-It" Verse:

"Rather, we have renounced secret and shameful ways; we do not use deception, nor do we distort the word of God. On the contrary, by setting forth the truth plainly we commend ourselves to every man's conscience in the sight of God."
2 Corinthians 4:2

"The Lord your God is with you, He is mighty to save.
He will take great delight in you, He will quiet you with
His love, He will rejoice over you with singing."
Zephaniah 3:17

24 - God is Happy

God is Happy If...

God is happy. How does that thought strike you? We tend to think that God is only happy *if*. God is only happy IF we please Him somehow. God is only happy IF we don't do anything to anger Him. We often assume His happiness is conditional, based on our behavior.

Does it seem odd to think that God is happy? Is happiness only something to be experienced by children or a bride on her wedding day? Can God be happy? Or is happiness something too trivial for Him? Can the Creator, Sustainer, Almighty God be happy, or is He too focused on His responsibilities and aware of the world the way it is?

The world does not see God as happy; in fact, quite the opposite. The world sees Him perpetually unhappy, grousing, and irritated by the burden that we have become to Him. To millions, God is seen as someone whose patience is always at the breaking point. He is angry, fed-up, frustrated, annoyed, and maybe even a bit regretful that He even created us in the first place.

Movies and media reinforce the idea that God is continually disappointed and unhappy with us. He is often characterized as sitting on a cloud, exasperated by all that He is witnessing, waiting for someone to do something that is so egregious that He must now finally take action. This action usually involves a lightning bolt of some kind.

The Problem of an Unhappy God

We are not drawn to unhappy people. The truth is, we try to avoid them if at all possible. This is also true of God. The misconception about the unhappiness of God may be one of the bigger reasons why non-believers often keep God at arm's length or are unwilling to embrace Him.

Christians are not immune to thinking of God in these terms. Believers also don't realize that God is happy. I asked thirty Christian friends to write down twenty words that describe God. *Happy* never made the list. Joyful was listed by one person. (*Just* made the list sixteen times; *wrathful* twice; *angry*, *vengeful*, and *stern* were each listed once.) But when we as His children think of God as unhappy, our relationship with Him is negatively affected.

You May Not Be, But God Is

When I told a friend I was taking the survey to see if anyone would describe God as *happy*, she immediately replied, "God's not happy."

Many bristle at using the word *happy* to describe God because feelings of happiness come and go so quickly. But the truth is OUR happiness comes and goes so quickly, not God's. We cannot let our experience of the fickleness of happiness discount the use of the word to describe God.

We may think or assume that God is unhappy, but what do the Scriptures reveal to us about God's happiness? From cover to cover in the Scriptures, quite literally from Genesis to Revelation, we can see that God is happy.

Evidence from Scripture

Genesis

Let's start at the very beginning. Was God happy when He first walked with Adam and Eve in the Garden? God looked at all He had made and declared it good, but He declared Adam and Eve very good. I think we can assume that God was happy walking and having fellowship with those whom He had made in His own image. We have no indication to think otherwise.

Does God change? Earlier we discussed the attribute of His unchangeableness (His immutability). If God cannot change, then He is still happy, even after the introduction of sin. God's self-sufficiency would dictate to us that God remained happy after the Fall of humanity in the Garden of Eden.

Old Testament Prophets

We often think of the prophets themselves as being unhappy characters; after all, their very role was often to chastise and warn the people of their coming judgment, punishment, and doom. But even as they spoke for God, they also spoke of His character. Isaiah wrote:

> "As a young man marries a maiden, so will your
> sons marry you; as a bridegroom rejoices over
> his bride, so will your God rejoice over you."
> (Isaiah 62:5)

Zephaniah also wrote of a happy and rejoicing Old Testament God:

> "The Lord your God is in your midst, a victorious warrior.
> He will exult over you with joy, He will be quiet in His
> love, He will rejoice over you with shouts of joy.
> (Zephaniah 3:17 NASB)

The Gospels

The Bible repeatedly testifies to the joy and happiness of God. Pastor and author, John Piper, has recognized and celebrated this attribute of God probably more than anyone else. The first chapter of his book, *Desiring God,* is titled "The Happiness of God." He has made it a focal point of his ministry to explain what the happiness of God means to us. He recognizes that God is happy because He is glorious. But the best news is that He invites us to enter into His happiness. Piper explains the happiness of God this way:

> "It is good news that God is gloriously happy. No one would want
> to spend eternity with an unhappy God. If God is unhappy then
> the goal of the gospel is not a happy goal, and that means it would
> be no gospel at all. But, in fact, Jesus invites us to spend eternity
> with a happy God when He says, 'Enter into the **joy** of your
> master' (Matthew 25:23). Jesus lived and died that His joy – **God's
> joy** – might be in us and our joy might be full (John 15:11; 17:13).
> Therefore the gospel is '**the gospel of the glory of the happy
> God.**'"[1]

Jesus asks us to imitate Him; to be like Him is the goal of every disciple. He desires His followers to have a full measure of the joy that He has.

> "I am coming to you now, but I say these things
> while I am still in the world, so that they may
> have the full measure of My joy within them."
> (John 17:13)

Acts

Unhappiness is the result of dissatisfaction; dissatisfaction is the result of needs not being met. God has no unmet needs. One can argue that because God is omniscient, He also has no unmet expectations. When Paul spoke at the Areopagus in Athens, he said:

> "The God who made the world and everything in it is the Lord of
> heaven and earth and does not live in temples built by hands. And

160

He is not served by human hands, as if He needed anything, because He Himself gives all men life and breath and everything else." (Acts 17:24-25)

If God has any unmet needs, He then ceases to be God. If God is to be God, He must be satisfied. God cannot be perfect and unhappy at the same time. Technically, by definition, God has to be happy.

Epistles

God commands us to be joyful. "Be joyful always" (1 Thessalonians 5:16). It would be hypocritical of God to ask us to be something that He is not.

Paul used an interesting word to describe God in his first letter to Timothy. He wrote:

> "We also know that the law is made not for the righteous but for lawbreakers and rebels, the ungodly and sinful, the unholy and irreligious, for those who kill their fathers or mothers, for murderers, for the sexually immoral, for those practicing homosexuality, for slave traders and liars and perjurers – and for whatever else is contrary to the sound doctrine that conforms to the gospel concerning the glory of the **blessed** God, which He entrusted to me."
> (1 Timothy 1:9-11)

In 1 Timothy, Paul wrote "the glorious gospel of the blessed God" (1:11), and later, "the blessed and only Sovereign" (6:15). The word *blessed* is the same word used in the beatitudes when Jesus said, "Blessed are those who..." in the Sermon on the Mount (Matthew 5:3-11). In both places the word is not *eulogētos* (translated as "blessed") but *makarios* which is properly translated as "happy."

Here Paul was making a statement not only about the gospel, but about God as well. He was telling us that God is happy (*makarios*). It was inconceivable to Paul that God could be denied infinite joy and still be all-glorious. His glory and His happiness are tied together. To be infinitely glorious is to also be infinitely happy. Day and night, never stopping, heavenly creatures sing of God that He is "Holy, Holy, Holy" – not that He is "Unhappy, Unhappy, Unhappy."

Revelation

God is eternal, so He sees all events (past, present, and future) equally vivid. He sees and is currently experiencing our future. In His "now" evil is being judged and defeated (Revelation 20:1-15). He doesn't just see current sin and rebellion and its tragic consequences; He also sees the future where every knee is bowing and every tongue is confessing Him to be Lord (Romans 14:11). God can be happy because He sees and experiences the ultimate victory over evil that we await with great anticipation.

The Joy and Happiness Problem
Now you may say at this point, "I agree that God is joyful, but the word *happy* is still not a good fit for me." It is true, the verses just cited in Matthew and John say God has joy (or is joyful); there is no verse that says God is happy.

What is the difference between joy and happiness? To us, joy is a deep-seated feeling of lasting contentment, hope, and gladness. God commands His people to be full of joy in Romans 12:12 and 1 Thessalonians 5:16. If joy were an emotion based upon circumstances, then that command would seem rather harsh and unrealistic. We may be joyful even in very difficult situations.

Our happiness comes and goes, sometimes rather quickly. We may be happy one moment and sad the next. Unlike joy, our happiness is largely based on our circumstances. If the good is currently outweighing the bad, we are happy, and vice versa.

But God is not affected by His (or our) circumstances. He is always joyful, so He is also always happy. His happiness is the result of His joy; it does not come and go like our happiness does.

The Happiness and Sin Problem
How can God be happy in the presence of so much sin? Is God happy about the state of the world? Isn't God grieved by what He sees every day? How does a righteous and just (or even wrathful) God remain happy?

God is not happy about our sin. It does grieve Him, but our sin does not affect His state of being. At this point it may be helpful to remember a previous quote from Tozer regarding the self-sufficiency of God: "Were every man on earth to become an atheist, it could not affect Him in any way."[2]

God is not like us. Our emotions affect our hearts. God can experience emotions but not be affected by them the same way as we are. Elihu made this point clear to his friend Job when he said:

"If you sin, how does that affect Him? If your sins are many,

what does that do to Him? If you are righteous, what do you
give to Him, or what does He receive from your hand?
Your wickedness affects only a man like yourself,
and your righteousness only the sons of men."
(Job 35:6-8)

The Divine Perspective on Sin and Evil

The great theologian, Jonathan Edwards, also struggled with this co-existence: "How can we affirm the happiness of God on the basis of His sovereignty when much of what God permits is contrary to His own commands in Scripture?" Piper summarizes Edwards's resolution to the question this way:

> "The infinite complexity of the divine mind is such that God has the capacity to look at the world through two lenses. He can look through a narrow lens or through a wide angle lens. When God looks at a painful or wicked event through His narrow lens, He sees the tragedy or the sin for what it is in itself and He is angered and grieved. But when God looks at a painful or wicked event through His wide-angle lens, He sees the tragedy or the sin in relation to everything leading up to it and everything flowing out from it. He sees it in relation to all the connections and effects that form a pattern or mosaic stretching into eternity."[3]

God is able to see the sin and suffering of this world and yet remain happy because He recognizes their eternal purpose. He allows sin and suffering to exist in order to accomplish His sovereign will. Admittedly, this boggles our understanding of how God providentially is at work in this world.

Another example may be of some help. When you are driving your car down the road, your eyes and your attention are either on the road ahead, looking at traffic, or they can be focused on the speedometer. You cannot give equal attention to both at the same time; it's impossible. You can try, but there is always a moment of transition from one to another. You have a limited ability to see the near and the far simultaneously.

God does not have this same limitation. He can and does see the sins of the world (through a narrow lens) and He is grieved. But at the same time, He can still see the full horizon (through a wide angle lens) and all the glory that lies ahead for those who will spend eternity with Him.

Again, the old refrain comes into play – God is not like us. Let's not assume His experiences and perspectives are the same as ours. To us, our joy and happiness look the same – until the storms come. To us, the Fruits of the Spirit often lay latent within us – until the opposite appears. Our superficial joy (our happiness) and real joy look exactly the same until the storm comes and blows one of them away. God is not like that; He is unaffected by the storms.

Why "God is Happy" is a BIG DEAL

You do not need to worry about God's emotional state. He has no regrets of creating us; in fact, the very opposite is true. He loves being God. He "delights fully in Himself and in all that reflects His character."[4] He takes great pleasure in all that He does. He loves us and is enthusiastic about serving His people and working for our welfare.

God invites us to join Him in His happiness. His desire is to share His happiness with you. Your welfare and even your happiness are a great concern to God.

> "If you keep My commands, you will remain in My love,
> just as I have kept my Father's commands and remain
> in His love. I have told you this so that My joy may
> be in you and that your joy may be complete."
> (John 15:10-11)

We now have hope. If God were not happy, we would be lost and without promise. Hope is a great thing, something we all need more of. Our hope in God is found in a God of great joy.

> "And if our Father's heart is full of deep and unshakable
> happiness, we may be sure that when we seek our happiness in
> Him we will not find Him 'out of sorts' when we come. We will
> not find a frustrated, gloomy, irritable Father who wants to be left
> alone, but instead a Father whose heart is so full of joy it spills
> over onto all those who are thirsty."[5]

God created us with desire for happiness because He knew it could only be satisfied in Him. We all desire to be happy. We live for comfort, security, and control. Almost every decision we make, whether conscious or not, revolves on what will make us happy. Blaise Pascal famously wrote:

> "All men seek happiness. This is without exception. Whatever
> different means they employ, they all tend to this end. The cause
> of some going to war, and of others avoiding it, is the same desire
> in both, attended with different views. The will never takes the

least step but to this object. This is the motive of every action of every man, even of those who hang themselves."[6]

God created us with this desire for happiness because He knew it could only be satisfied in Him. The challenge for us all is to consider where we are looking for happiness and lasting contentment. Most find a measure of temporal satisfaction and escape in the fleeting pleasures of this world. How we respond to this desire for happiness is the issue. We must either turn to God or to the things of this world.

As we experience satisfaction in God, we work out our salvation in ever-increasing levels of refinement. Our Christ-likeness comes into clearer focus when we determine to walk by faith and live for God's glory alone.

God is most glorified when we are most satisfied in Him (when we are happy in Him).

"If God were not infinitely devoted to the preservation, display, and enjoyment of His own glory, we could have no hope of finding happiness in Him. But if He does in fact employ all His sovereign power and infinite wisdom to maximize the enjoyment of His own glory, then we have a foundation on which to stand and rejoice."[7]

The joy of the Lord, the happiness of God, is the ultimate source of our fulfillment. God desires us to be happy because He himself is happy, and this happens best when we seek only His glory. In Christ alone is lasting happiness found. God desires more than for us to simply enjoy Him and His happiness; His desire is to be glorified, which is His highest happiness.

God desires for His people to be strong in Him, so He graciously gives us joy as we cooperate with Him in our sanctification. "Do not grieve, for the joy of the Lord is your strength" (Nehemiah 8:10).

Our joy and happiness is …
    the result of our daily walk and relationship with the Lord.

Our joy and happiness is …
    found in continual recognition of our daily blessings and spiritual standing.

Our joy and happiness is …
    our source of strength for living lives that are obedient to His desires.

Reflection Questions:

1. What is your default opinion – is God happy or not?
2. Why is the happiness of God a permanent trait and not a passing mood that God experiences?
3. Which of the evidences from Scripture did you appreciate the most?
4. In what is your happiness found – your circumstances or your standing with God?
5. What holds you back from seeking your happiness in God?
6. What would it say about God if He were not happy or if His mood changed?
7. Because God is happy, I will . . .

"Think-On-It" Verse:

"I have told you this so that My joy may be
in you and that your joy may be complete."
John 15:11

> "My sheep listen to My voice; I know
> them, and they follow Me."
> John 10:27-29

25 - God is Relational

Where's My Car?

When I was in high school I had a job carrying out groceries at a local supermarket. One day I came home complaining about all the "stupid people" I had run into that day – some of them, literally. I was irritated that some felt the need to tell me how to pack their bags. People were seemingly always in my way. Or to top it off, because they couldn't remember where they parked their car, they then often led me up and down the rows of the parking lot in search of their lost vehicle.

After my little rant, my dad said something that I have always remembered. He said something like, "You know, all these people you are complaining about are created in God's image." His point was clear; by complaining about "stupid people" I was complaining about God's creation – and not just any creation, but the very thing that He had created in His own image.

Created for Relationship

Being created in God's image means many things. One of the most important is that we are created for relationship with Him. We are very different from anything else God created. We are created in His image. We are created like Him in many respects.

The world largely misses this point. Ingrid Newkirk, the co-founder of People for the Ethical Treatment of Animals (PETA), is quoted as saying, "There is no rational basis for saying that a human being has special rights. A rat is a pig is a dog is a boy. They're all mammals."[1]

If creator-less evolution is true, she's right. Without God, we are all equal creatures and nothing distinguishes your son or daughter from a rat or a pig or a dog. But there is a huge difference between a rat, a pig, a dog, and a child. Animals are not created in the image of God; children are.

When the Scripture states, "Let Us make man in Our image, in Our likeness" (Genesis 1:26), there is a clear understanding that to the original readers this simply meant, "Let Us make man to be *like* Us and to *represent* Us."[2] It's clear from the text that this latest creation was very different from anything else previously created. These humans were to be like Him and to represent Him here on earth.

Many may wish the verse would then go on to explain exactly what this means. What does it mean exactly to be like God? We would love to have a defined list of qualities and attributes that we share with our Creator. But compiling an exhaustive list of the ways that we are like God isn't possible. In fact, any effort would never come close to doing justice on the topic.

Genesis only needs to reaffirm that we are like God. The rest of the Bible fills in the details to better explain how. An exhaustive understanding of our likeness to God is also not possible because it would require a complete and comprehensive understanding of who God is.[3]

Evidence of Attributes Shared with Our Creator

Being created in God's image means we share some attributes with Him in a limited way. These shared attributes allow us to experience God in relationship.

Morally – We inherently know right from wrong. No one has to tell you that pushing Grandma down the stairs is a bad idea. We have an inner sense that some behavior is wrong (and sinful). This inner sense then makes us morally accountable before God for our actions.

Spiritually – We have physical bodies, but we also have immaterial spirits. We have spiritual lives that allow us to relate to God, to pray to Him, to praise Him, and to hear Him speaking to us. You can pray for your pets, but your pets cannot pray for you.

Mentally – We have the ability to reason and think logically. Animals have been able to learn and solve rudimentary mazes and problems, but they do not engage in abstract thought. Chimps may have ridden inside our spaceships, but they never designed or built any of them.

Socially – We have the ability to experience intimate and interpersonal harmony with each other through friendship, family, and marriage. Animals can experience community together, but not the depth of relationship that people enjoy. We also have the awareness that a relationship with God is possible.

Eternally Perfect and Non-Perfect Relationships

It may sound awkward, but for all of eternity God has been in perfect relationship with Himself. God is a Trinity of three distinct persons: Father, Son, and Spirit. He has always existed in this perfect and completely self-sufficient relationship.

Then He made us. Since then, things have gotten a bit more complicated. With our creation came the opportunity for us to enjoy Him in a temporarily non-perfect relationship. While we walk this earth, we have a chance to walk in relationship with God through the person of Christ. Although eternally content with Himself, God now desires to be known by us and to have relationship with us. Our relationship with Him will never be perfect this side of heaven, but an eternally perfect relationship with God awaits those who believe.

Infinite and Intimate

When we spoke on the infinite nature of God at the beginning of this book, I mentioned that God is both infinite and intimate. That intimacy is found in the fact that God is relational and personal.

> "In the teaching of the Bible, God is both infinite and personal: He is infinite in that He is not subject to any of the limitations of humanity, or of creation in general. He is far greater than everything He has made, far greater than anything else that exists. But He is also personal: He interacts with us as a person and we can relate to Him as persons. We can pray to Him, worship Him, obey Him, and love Him, and He can speak to us, rejoice in us, and love us."[4]

This personal and intimate nature separates the God of the Bible from all the other gods and religious systems of this world. We serve a God who cares for and dearly loves His people in both the collective and individual sense. In fact, we are continually portrayed as His children throughout the Scriptures (Ephesians 1:5, 2:19, 5:1, 8; 1 Peter 4:16; Galatians 3:26, 4:6-7; Romans 8:15-17).

Greek and Roman gods of mythology were personal in nature. They interacted with people, displayed weaknesses, and even experienced their own failures from time to time. They were personal, but they were not infinite or unlimited. Conversely, deists believe that God is infinite and all-powerful but often fail to recognize His personal and intimate nature. The key to an accurate and Biblical understanding of God is seeing Him with a proper balance of His infinite and intimate nature. He is both all powerful and personal at the same time.

God Came to Dwell with Us, Not Just to Help Us

God's pursuit of deep, intimate relationship with His people is the central theme of the Bible. In fact, the ultimate expression of God's relational pursuit of us is the person of Jesus Christ. The Old Testament prophesies that ...

> "Therefore the Lord Himself will give you a sign:
> The virgin will be with child and will give birth
> to a son, and will call Him Immanuel."
> (Isaiah 7:14)

The name Immanuel is translated, "God with us." The importance is not simply the fact that God exists, but that He exists *with* His creation. He is with us. He is here not just when we need Him, but each and every day. God did not send His Son to only provide us a way of salvation. He did not send His Holy Spirit to only help us as a counselor. God's desire is to dwell with us.

It Gets Better ... God Came to Dwell *In* Us, Not Just *With* Us

Before Jesus left His friends to fend for themselves; He promised to send them someone who would be with them forever. In fact, He said it was better for them that He would leave and that this "someone else" would come. That someone else was the person of the Holy Spirit.

> "But I tell you the truth: It is for your good that I am
> going away. Unless I go away, the Counselor will not
> come to you; but if I go, I will send Him to you."
> (John 16:7)

The promise is given again after the resurrection (John 20:21-22, Acts 1:4-7) and fulfilled in the opening chapters of Acts. God walked with us as Immanuel and then promised to come back to dwell *within* us through the person of the Holy Spirit. Paul spoke of this indwelling presence of the Holy Spirit often.

> "Don't you know that you yourselves are God's temple and
> that God's Spirit lives in you?" "Do you not know that your
> body is a temple of the Holy Spirit, who is in you, whom
> you have received from God? You are not your own."
> (1 Corinthians 3:16, 6:19)

> "Do not get drunk on wine, which leads to
> debauchery. Instead, be filled with the Spirit."
> (Ephesians 5:18)

170

While the Old Testament predicts and promises the coming "Immanuel," the New Testament explains the implications of a relational God in much greater detail. To the church in Galatia, Paul wrote on the significance of having a God that dwells within us in light of the cross of Christ.

> "I have been crucified with Christ and I
> no longer live, but Christ lives in me."
> (Galatians 2:20)

I have always found this idea of being crucified with Christ to be a confusing one. Chris Tiegreen explains this somewhat complicated idea in his daily devotional writing:

> "Jesus did not come to us and promise to show us the way, to feed us the bread, to shine the light on us, to tell us the truth, or any other such direct assistance. No, He is much closer to us than that. He does not just offer us these things; He *is* these things. In a very real and literal way, Jesus is our life now. We do not ask Him for His help in living our lives; we ask Him to live His life more profoundly (in us), more transparently each day. That is why it is never appropriate simply to see Him as our Teacher, Guide, Counselor, Healer, Deliverer, and the like, insofar as we think these roles belong to a person outside of ourselves. He is genuinely in the depths of our heart, asking us to get the junk out of the way for Him to shine through us. We are crucified; He is alive."[5]

God's desires for us are much deeper than we realize. He is not here to help us, but to dwell within us. He already knows us; His desire is for us to know Him – not to know more *about* Him but to know *Him* in a personal, relational, and even intimate way.

Why "God is Relational" is a BIG DEAL

You have great value as an image bearer of God. Your worth is based on who you are, not on what you do. You have a stamp upon you that reads, "Made by God – Made like God – Made for God." That alone gives you value, worth, and dignity that you may not realize.

Everyone is worthy of respect and dignity because even the worst sinner is still an image bearer of God. This truth that we all are image bearers fuels the passion and commitment for those who fight to defend the unborn and stand up for the rights of the disabled.

This understanding also leaves us with a God-honoring burden to care for the orphaned children in Africa, Haiti, and throughout the world. Whether an AIDS orphan, a Down Syndrome child, or a paralyzed adult on life support, all have worth and value not always realized by the society at large.

You can now experience peace from His presence. When you recognize a relationship with God is possible, you realize a peace and reassurance in your life that only God can provide.

> "Do not be anxious about anything, but in everything, by prayer
> and petition, with thanksgiving, present your requests to God.
> And the peace of God, which transcends all understanding,
> will guard your hearts and your minds in Christ Jesus."
> (Philippians 4:4-7)

You still have relational responsibilities. God enables relationship with Him through our faith, but like any relationship, this one also requires some effort (and discipline) on our part as well. Simply living and breathing and walking the planet each day does not allow you to experience God in relationship. There is also an element of action that is required on our part to walk in daily relationship with our God.

A Growing Relationship with God requires ...
- Sacrificial Living (Genesis 12:1, 22:3; Mark 8:34-38)
- Purity (Numbers 19:17; Psalm 24:4; 1 Thessalonians 4:3-5)
- A Right Heart (Psalm 4:4; Isaiah 1:16; Daniel 7:28; Micah 6:6-8)
- Obedience (2 Chronicles 34:32; Job 41:11; 1 Peter 1:13-16)
- Worship (2 Samuel 6:5; Psalms 105:4, 147:1; John 4:27)

God desires to communicate with you in this relationship. God has wired us for two-way communication, not just one-sided prayer. Most often, if we're not careful, prayer becomes only a time of us talking *to* God and spending very little (if any) time *listening to* Him. God speaks. We don't often hear Him very well, but He speaks and calls out to us.

In addition to the revelation of Himself through the Bible (which is the most comprehensive revelation of Himself), God speaks to us in an effort to build our relationship with Him in several ways.

First, *God speaks through our invitation for salvation.* If you are a believer in Christ and have accepted Him as your Savior, you have heard God's voice. He has called you to join His family. You have heard and accepted that call to salvation.

"No one can come to Me unless the
Father who sent Me draws him…"
(John 6:44)

Second, *God speaks through others.* Has God ever spoken to your heart through a speaker, pastor, writer, sermon, podcast, Christian radio program, godly friend or Bible study leader? If you are learning anything about God while reading this book, God is speaking truth to you.

Third, *God speaks to us through worship.* When we worship God on Sunday or even find ourselves listening to God-honoring music in our cars, we are allowing Him to speak to us and minister to our hearts and minds. God speaks to us in song and lyric and anything else we may do to show Him worth.

Fourth, *God speaks by convicting us of what is wrong and convincing us of what is right.* Why do you feel guilty when you have sinned? It's because God is speaking to you. He is telling you that something is wrong and interfering in your relationship with Him.

"When He comes, He will convict the world of guilt
in regard to sin and righteousness and judgment."
(John 16:8)

The opposite is also true, God is also here to convince us of what is true and what is right. God desires to tell you what He loves and appreciates about you.

"But when He, the Spirit of truth, comes, He will guide you into
all truth. He will not speak on His own; He will speak only
what He hears, and He will tell you what is yet to come."
(John 16:13)

Fifth, *God speaks through the prompting of His Holy Spirit.* Have you ever felt an urge to pray for someone? Have you ever sensed God prompting you in any way? Have you ever heard His voice or sensed His leading to do something specific?

Some believers may grow a bit apprehensive when the conversation turns to "hearing God's voice." And it is necessary to point out that discerning God's voice always requires two things:

1st - A testing and weighing of Scripture: Does God's prompting align itself with the truth of His Word? God only speaks truth and never says anything contrary to the Scriptures.

2ⁿᵈ - We must live in relationship with others: When we sense God's leading or prompting, it's important to ask godly friends if they see any validity to what we may have heard God say. We are to live with the guidance, counsel, and accountability of other believers.

Reflection Questions:

1. What aspects of your own creation do you need to have more of an appreciation for?
2. What comfort can be found in the fact that God is relational by nature?
3. Do you see God as someone who is here only to help you or to actually dwell within you?
4. Ask God, is there anything He wants to correct in you, or anything you need to confess – or ask forgiveness for?
5. Ask God, what has pleased Him about you lately?
6. Ask God, is there someone you need to encourage? Who?
7. Because God is relational, I will . . .

"Think-On-It" Verse:

"O Jerusalem, Jerusalem, you who kill the prophets and stone those sent to you, how often I have longed to gather your children together, as a hen gathers her chicks under her wings, but you were not willing."
Matthew 23:37

"We know that we live in Him and He in us, because He has given us of His Spirit. And we have seen and testify that the Father has sent His Son to be the Savior of the world. If anyone acknowledges that Jesus is the Son of God, God lives in him and he in God."
1 John 4:13-15

The Conclusion: It Makes a Difference

Knowing and meditating on God's character brings peace and reassurance to our lives. Soon after finishing up the rough draft of the final attribute, I found myself lying in bed worrying about the issues that life throws at each of us on occasion. I just finished writing about God's faithfulness, goodness, and sovereignty, and there I lay, worrying about upcoming bills and a flooded basement.

At 2:30 a.m. I was confronted with this question: Do I believe all that I've just written? I realized throughout the writing process that it's easier to put something down on paper than to live it out.

The answer is yes, I do believe all that I've written – in my head. But spiritual maturity is the life-long process of your heart catching up to what you believe in your head to be true. Our hearts are not always at peace even though we *know* the truth.

We may believe in these attributes of God, but far too often we live our daily lives as if they were not true.

If you've read this book in a peaceful and abundant season of your life, you might find it easy to agree with everything you've read. But chances are you will experience trials and stressful times in the days or years ahead, and at that point you may question the love, sovereignty, faithfulness, and goodness of God.

A sovereign God allows difficult times because we are drawn to know Him more intimately when we need Him most. The next time you find yourself troubled by the situations of life, ask yourself, "Which of God's attributes am I not believing in right now?"

You may *feel* like God has withheld His sovereignty, His goodness, or His faithfulness in your situation. At that point the choice is yours. You can choose to believe what you know to be true or choose to follow your own thoughts and feelings. This is the battle we all fight every day.

Changing the way we think is not an easy task. Those who study the function of the brain tell us that renewed thinking, or changing old thinking patterns, is a neurological challenge as well as a practical one.

Fortunately, the Scriptures help us with this challenge by inviting us to make the decision to think on the things of God. Paul wrote of this often in his letters to those experiencing new life in Christ.

> "Those who live according to the flesh have their *minds* set on what the flesh desires; but those who live in accordance with the Spirit have their *minds* set on what the Spirit desires. The *mind* governed by the flesh is death, but **the mind governed by the Spirit is life and peace.** The *mind* governed by the flesh is hostile to God; it does not submit to God's law, nor can it do so. Those who are in the realm of the flesh cannot please God."
> (Romans 8:5-8)

> "Do not conform any longer to the pattern of this world, but be transformed by the **renewing of your mind.**"
> (Romans 12:2)

> "Do not be anxious about anything, but in everything, by prayer and petition, with thanksgiving, present your requests to God. And the peace of God, which transcends all understanding, will guard your hearts and your *minds* in Christ Jesus. Whatever is true, whatever is noble, whatever is right, whatever is pure, whatever is lovely, whatever is admirable – *if anything is excellent or praiseworthy* – **think about such things.**"
> (Philippians 4:6-8)

> "Set your **minds** on things above, not on earthly things."
> (Colossians 3:20)

The choice is always yours – to think on the things of God or to follow your own thoughts and focus on your circumstances. Make no mistake about it – in the short run, this is the easier of the two options; that's why most of the world follows this path.

It's easier to complain, be anxious, and blame God than it is to change your thinking and submit to His will. While this path may be easier in the short run, ultimately this choice breeds only more unhappiness, doubt, and fear.

We experience God in relationship, not just by having more knowledge about Him. Knowing more *about* God doesn't necessarily mean you will *experience* Him. It's a great start, but it's just that – a start.

"God is glorified in His people by the way we experience Him, not merely the way we think about Him. Indeed the devil thinks more true thoughts about God in one day than a saint does in a lifetime, and God is not honored by it. The problem with the devil is not his theology, but his desires. Our chief end is to glorify God, the great Object. We do so most fully when we treasure Him, desire Him, delight in Him so supremely that we let goods and kindred go and display His love to the poor and the lost."[1]

In other words, the stupidest demon can read every theology book ever written and still point out the things that were not mentioned. Knowing more about God is a great start – a necessary start. But knowing *about* Him and truly knowing *Him* are two very different things.

One is an issue of the mind; the other, an issue of the heart. Ask God to invade your heart, and then run hard after Him. The study of God's Word and learning more about Him is vitally important, but so is recognizing that a relationship with Christ brings a new life.

"Therefore, if anyone is in Christ, the new creation
has come: The old has gone, the new is here!"
(2 Corinthians 5:17)

We make wiser decisions and live holier lives when we know more about God. Wisdom begins with a knowledge of who God is. The challenge is to live a wiser life with what you now know. It's both sad and amazing that so many professors can teach the Bible as literature but still live unrepentant lives.

It's both sad and quite sobering that so many churches have drifted from the truth taught in the Scriptures to a new "truth" that is more palatable and acceptable to society.

Knowledge does not save you. Your knowledge isn't everything. In fact, it's worthless when it's not applied. Hopefully, you now have more knowledge about God, but how it will affect your life is up to you. Take what you know about God and use it to live differently.

Because God is ...

Infinite – start thinking bigger thoughts about Him.
Holy – live a life that is pure and pleasing to Him.
Loving – go and love others sacrificially.
Merciful – show mercy to those in need.
Gracious – be generous and giving to others.
Righteous – trust that justice will be done someday.
All Present – enjoy His presence wherever you are.
All Powerful – pray bigger prayers.
All Knowing – trust that He knows your situation.
Transcendent – be in awe of His majesty.
Unchanging – have confidence that He is there.
Sovereign – know that He is always in charge.
Self-Existent – realize He is bigger than your needs.
Self-Sufficient – recognize the honor of serving Him.
Wise – live by His teachings.
Faithful – know He will always be true.
Good – remember His plans are best.
Forgiving – forgive those who hurt you.
Eternal – remember He sees your past pain clearly.
Jealous – be aware of your affections.
Humble – do not think too highly of yourself.
Patient – show patience with others.
Truth – don't let the world pull you elsewhere.
Happy – be joyful.
Relational – enjoy relationship with Him!

Extra Stuff: The Appendix

Extra Stuff: Reading & Recording Log

After reading an attribute, record the main point to remember.

Infinite _____

Holy _____

Loving _____

Merciful _____

Gracious _____

Righteous _____

All Present _____

All Powerful _____

All Knowing _____

Transcendent _____

Unchanging _____

Sovereign _____

Self-Existent _____

Self-Sufficient _____

Wise _____

Faithful _____

Good _____

Forgiving _____

Eternal _____

Jealous _____

Humble _____

Patient _____

Truth _____

Happy _____

Relational _____

Extra Stuff: God is Unchanging
"Does God Change His Mind?"

These verses make the case that God is unchanging and unchangeable.

> "Every good and perfect gift is from above,
> coming down from the Father of the heavenly lights,
> who does not change like shifting shadows."
> (James 1:17)

> "God is not a man, that He should lie, nor a son of man,
> that He should change His mind. Does He speak and
> then not act? Does He promise and not fulfill?"
> (Numbers 23:19)

However, this appears to contradict what is taught in other verses:

> "The Lord was grieved that He had made man on the earth ..."
> (Genesis 6:6)

> "When God saw what they did and how they turned
> from their evil ways, He had compassion and did not
> bring upon them the destruction He had threatened."
> (Jonah 3:10)

> "Then the Lord relented and did not bring on
> His people the disaster He had threatened."
> (Exodus 32:14)

Does God Really Repent?

These verses speak of the Lord repenting of something, and seem contrary to passages that tell us that God is unchanging, but a closer look shows us that God is not capable of changing His mind.

In the original language, the word that is translated as *repent* or *relent* is the Hebrew expression of "to be sorry for." Being sorry for something does not mean that a change has occurred; it simply means that there is regret for something that has taken place.

When the Scriptures say, "The Lord was grieved that He had made man on the earth," this simply means that God felt some sorrow for creating man. At this point we need to remember that God is omniscient. God knew He would feel this way even while He was creating us. He was not surprised by the events of Genesis 6.

While He was grieved by sin, He did not reverse His decision. Instead, He used Noah to allow for our continued existence. The fact that we are alive today is proof that God did not change His mind about creating us. Also, take note that it was our sinfulness that triggered God's sorrow, not our existence.

God Responds Differently to Different Situations

In the book of Jonah we read,

> "When God saw what they did and how they turned from their evil ways, He had compassion and did not bring upon them the destruction He had threatened."
>
> Jonah 3:10

It might seem as if God had changed His mind when He decided to spare the Ninevites, but the truth is, the people of Ninevah had changed by repenting. Jonah was told to preach for a reason. God is consistent, He was going to judge Nineveh because of its evil; however, the Ninevites repented and changed *their* ways. As a result, God had mercy on Nineveh, which is entirely consistent with His character.

Did the change on the part of the Ninevites obligate God to act as He did? No. God cannot be placed in a position of obligation to us. God is good and righteous. He chose not to punish the Ninevites as a result of their change of heart. If anything, this passage points to the fact that God does not change. Had He not preserved the Ninevites, His action of judgment would have been contrary to His character.

The Scriptures that describe God as changing His mind are human attempts to explain the actions of God. He was going to do something, but instead did something else. To us, that sounds like a change. But to God, who is omniscient, it is not a change. God always knew what He was going to do.

God threatened Nineveh with destruction, knowing that it would cause Nineveh to repent. God threatened Israel with destruction, knowing that Moses would intercede. God does not regret His decisions. God does not change His mind, but rather acts consistently with His Word in response to our actions.

Edited and Amended from Got Questions.org - http://www.gotquestions.org/God-change-mind.html - June 5th, 2011

Extra Stuff: God is Truth
The Dangers of Postmodernism

Postmodernism is the belief that there is no objective or absolute truth, especially in matters of religion and spirituality. When confronted with a truth claim regarding the reality of God, postmodernism's viewpoint is exemplified in the statement, "that may be true for you, but not for me." This response is fine when you're discussing your favorite foods, but this way of thinking is dangerous when it confuses matters of opinion with truth.

Postmodernism is used to describe the current era which came after the age of modernism. It is the reaction to modernism's failure to use human reasoning to make the world a better place. Because one of modernism's beliefs was that absolutes did indeed exist, postmodernism seeks to correct things by eliminating absolute truth and making everything relative to an individual's beliefs and desires.

The dangers of postmodernism begin with the rejection of absolute truth. This quickly leads to a philosophy of religious pluralism that says no faith or religion is objectively true, which means no one can claim their religion is true and another is false.

Dangers of Postmodernism #1 – Relative Truth
For centuries God was considered the center of truth, but beginning with the Renaissance, thinkers began to elevate humankind to the center of reality. Renee Descartes' "I think, therefore I am" personified the beginning of this era. God was not the foundation of truth any longer; man now was.

The Enlightenment period brought the claim that only scientific data could be objectively understood, defined, and defended. Truth as it pertained to religion was discounted. Immanuel Kant argued that true knowledge about God was impossible, so he divided knowledge between facts and faith.

According to Kant, facts have nothing to do with religion. The result was that spiritual matters were seen as matters of the heart and opinion. Only the sciences were allowed to speak of truth. While modernism believed in absolutes of science, God's special revelation was excluded from the realm of truth.

Where Kant marked the transition from the Enlightenment to

183

modernism, Nietzsche symbolizes the shift from modernism to postmodernism. Nietzsche believed that all knowledge (including science) is a matter of perspective and interpretation. Many other philosophers have built upon Nietzsche's work and have shared his rejection of God and religion. They also rejected any hint of a truth that transcends all peoples and cultures (a meta-narrative).

This evolution of thought against objective truth has resulted in a complete aversion to any claim to absolutes. This naturally paints a bulls-eye on the Bible and its claim of inerrant truth.

Dangers of Postmodernism #2 – Loss of Discernment

If absolute truth does not exist, then everything is a matter of interpretation. To the postmodernists, even the author of a book does not possess the correct interpretation of their work; it is the reader who actually determines what the book is really about. Since there are a multitude of readers, but only one author, there are then multiple interpretations. As a result, there is no universally valid interpretation.

This is especially true in matters of faith once religion is assigned to the category of opinion. Our attempts to make distinctions in the area of religion (that one belief is right and another wrong) carry no more weight than one person arguing that chocolate is better than vanilla.

Dangers of Postmodernism #3 – Pluralism

If absolute truth does not exist and there is no way to make right or wrong distinctions between faiths, then the natural result is that all beliefs must be considered valid. The term for this is "philosophical pluralism," which means no religion has the right to pronounce itself true and another false.

The dangers of post-modernism are real and are imposing threats to Christianity because they relegate God's Word to something that has no authority over mankind and no ability to show itself as true in a world of competing religious voices. Christianity's claim that Christ is the only hope of salvation is rejected.

The Christian Response to Postmodernism

Christianity claims to be absolutely true and that matters of right and wrong do exist. It claims to be the truth in its assertions about God, and holds that contrary claims of other religions are false. This belief then leads to the accusation of intolerance. But truth is not a matter of preference, and when looked at closely, the foundations of postmodernism crumble and reveal Christianity's claims to be worthy and credible.

Postmodernism says that no truth should be affirmed, but this position is self-defeating. It affirms at least one absolute truth: that no absolute truth exists. Postmodernists do not believe in absolute truth, but they write books stating things they expect their readers to embrace as truth. "When someone says there is no such thing as truth, they are asking you not to believe them. So don't."

Christianity claims that differences exist between the Christian faith and others. But those claiming that meaningful distinctions do not exist between religions are actually making a distinction. They are attempting to show a difference in what they believe to be true and the Christian's truth claims.

Postmodernist authors expect their readers to come to the right conclusions about what they have written and will correct those who interpret their work differently than intended. Again, their philosophy proves itself to be self-defeating because they eagerly make distinctions between what they believe to be true and what they see as being false.

Finally, Christianity claims to be true in what it says about the sacrifice of Christ, our separation due to our sin, and our need for repentance. When Paul addressed the crowd in Athens, he said,

> "Therefore having overlooked the times
> of ignorance, God is now declaring to men
> that all people everywhere should repent."
> (Acts 17:30)

His declaration was not a "this is true for me, but may not be true for you" statement. It was a universal command from God to everyone. Those who argue against this are committing an error against their own philosophy that says no religion is incorrect. They are violating their own belief that every religion is equally true.

It's not arrogant for a math teacher to insist that $2 + 2 = 4$ or for a locksmith to insist that only one key will fit a lock. It's also equally reasonable for a Christian to insist that Christianity is true and anything opposed to it is false. Absolute truth does exist and there are consequences for being wrong. While pluralism may be popular in our temporary worldly matters, when it comes to the things that matter most, the truth of God is the most important thing there is to know.

Edited & Amended from GotQuestions.org - http://www.gotquestions.org/postmodernism-dangers.html - December 27th, 2010

Extra Stuff: God is Loving
What is a Covenant Relationship?

We have a love-based relationship with God, a covenant relationship. The problem is that we live our lives in a contract-oriented society. When we carry over this contract mentality into our covenant relationship with God, our understanding of that relationship can become a bit skewed. We do not have a contract with God; we have a covenant. Thankfully, there is a huge difference.

Contracts are for a limited period of time. When that time is up, the contract can then be resigned or extended with modifications. Contracts are also centered on specific and specified duties. For example, athletes are paid millions of dollars to play their sport; they are not expected to sweep up the stadium afterward.

A contract is based on a services rendered agreement. It is an if-then relationship. *If* I pay my cable TV bill, *then* I can continue to watch my shows. Contracts are motivated by the desire for both parties to get something they want. Both parties benefit from this agreement. Most often, one gets paid and the other gets what they paid for.

Covenant relationships are very different. Our relationship with God is not for a limited time or based on the exchange of an if-then principle. Other important differences include:

Covenants are initiated for the benefit of the *other*. God made a covenant with Noah to save him and his family. The agreement was not made in order to entice Noah's love or appreciation. A covenant relationship is a commitment to the *other's* well-being. God does not gain anything; He is not provided for or made better because of His covenant with us.

Covenant relationships are unconditional promises. There is no if-then agreement. For those in a saving relationship with God (those who have asked Christ to forgive them of their sins), there is no exchange of obedience for God's love. God does not love you more *if* you go to church or *if* you tithe.

Covenant relationships are based on steadfast love. You can (and often do) enter into contracts with complete strangers. We have no idea who the garbage man is or who runs the cable TV company.

God's covenant with us is based on God's love for us and our response to that love.

Covenant relationships are permanent. They do not expire. They are not set up for a designated period of time. They are not renegotiated or extended. They are made to last forever. We do not need to worry that our relationship with God can change without notice.

Covenant relationships require confrontation and forgiveness. Confrontation means holding the other person accountable for his words and actions when there is an offense. Our failures do not break our covenant with God, but we do need to ask Him for continual forgiveness to keep our relationship with Him abiding and growing. God will confront us when we have sinned and fallen short.

The South African writer, teacher, and pastor, Andrew Murray, wrote on the importance of those living in a covenant relationship with God to know the blessings found in it.

"Blessed is the man who truly knows God as his Covenant God; who knows what the Covenant promises him; what unwavering confidence of expectation it secures, that all its terms will be fulfilled to him; what a claim and hold it gives him on the Covenant-keeping God Himself. To many a man, who has never thought much of the Covenant, a true and living faith in it would mean the transformation of his whole life. *The full knowledge of what God wants to do* for him; *the assurance that it will be done* by an Almighty Power; *the being drawn to God Himself* in personal surrender, and dependence, and waiting to have it done; all this would make the Covenant the very gate of heaven. May the Holy Spirit give us some vision of its glory."

The Two Covenants Murray, Andrew (1828-1917) First published by London: J. Nisbet, 1899 Public Domain (Fort Washington, Pennsylvania: Christian Literature Crusade, 1974), p. 2.

Extra Stuff: God is Humble
A Call to Downward Mobility

Everybody wants to be somebody, and most of us long to be somebody more important than we are. Since the beginning we have been trying to move up the scale of importance. The first and best example may be the temptation of Adam and Eve.

"When you eat of the tree your eyes will be opened,
and you will be like God, knowing good and evil."
(Genesis 3:5)

Adam and Eve enjoyed the ultimate, sinless, love relationship with God, yet they desired something more. Henri Nouwen points out that ever since, we have been tempted to replace this love with power.
"The long painful history of the church is the history of people ever and again tempted to choose power over love, control over the cross, being a leader over being led."

This is a theme running throughout the Bible, throughout human history, and throughout our own experience. It's seen in the request of two disciples to be exalted and seated at the right and left of Jesus.

"Then James and John, the sons of Zebedee, came
to Him. 'Teacher,' they said, 'we want You to do for
us whatever we ask.' 'What do you want Me to do for
you?' He asked. They replied, 'Let one of us sit at
your right and the other at your left in your glory.'"
(Mark 10:35-37)

We shouldn't be surprised with James and John. While their bluntness makes them seem selfish, the motive of their request is not strange. Shared glory, honored positions, and closeness to powerful people are popular means of being somebody. If we can't be the one *with* the power, then being close to them is the next best thing. Their glory will make us look better; some of their honor may spill over onto us.

Jesus' response challenges the popular assumptions about greatness, power, and prominence:

"Can you drink the cup I drink or be baptized with the baptism
I am baptized with? Whoever wants to become great among
you must be your servant and whoever wants to be first must
be slave of all. For even the Son of Man did not come to be
served, but to serve, and to give His life as a ransom for many."
(Mark 10:38, 43-45)

The cup from which Jesus drank is self-emptying love, the giving of one's own life for others. The baptism of Christ brings death to the old way with its power games. It ushers in God's reign of justice, generosity, servanthood, and joy. This is downward mobility. It's the opposite of our hard wiring.

The world's image of greatness is hierarchical, with the greatest at the pinnacle of the pyramid and God hovering over the top. The closer one gets to the pinnacle, the closer one is to greatness and to the image of God. Success, upward mobility, and *being* served are signs of faithfulness to a hierarchical god.

The way of Jesus leads us in another direction, the opposite direction. Nouwen writes:

"The way of the Christian leader is not the way of upward mobility in which the world has invested so much, but the way of downward mobility ending on the cross. . . . It is not a leadership of power and control, but a leadership of powerlessness and humility in which the suffering servant of God, Jesus Christ, is made manifest."

Giving our lives as a ransom for many involves making ourselves available to others. It is offering our time, our energy, our money, our total being, our need of recognition, our ambition, and our humility.

James and John were selfish, but at least they knew where true greatness lay. They did not understand what they were asking, but they were asking the right person. They suspected that Jesus was the One who would come into glory, although they did not understand the full implication of their request.

Our desire to be noticed, appreciated, and more important than we are is our natural way of thinking. It mostly goes unnoticed by us until we are confronted by the model of humility taught and lived out before us by the God who humbled Himself to the point of becoming a man to live among us. We are to live like Christ: live downward.

Edited and Amended from an article by Kenneth L. Carder in *Christian Century*, Oct. 8, 1997, p. 869

Extra Stuff: God is Patient
Can You Really Disappoint God?

Can you disappoint God? Most people would say yes without thinking much about it. It's almost automatic to think that we can and often do disappoint God with our continual sinful thoughts, actions, and attitudes. After all, when we're disappointed with ourselves, it's easy to assume that God is also disappointed in us.

In many situations, disappointment infers a lack of patience to some degree. But how we answer this question may help us to better understand God's patience and, in turn, how we view God's patience may also influence our answer to this question. Take some time to consider these six points and not just assume the answer.

First, consider the meaning of the word *disappointment.* Disappointment is the result of an unfulfilled expectation. To be disappointed means that you expected one outcome but got another. So if God is disappointed, it would mean that something didn't happen that He was expecting to happen. God is omniscient; He knows everything. You can never surprise Him or do something unexpected.

Second, it might sound a bit strange, but God doesn't have any unmet expectations of you; He already knows what you *will* do for Him in the future.

> "For we are God's handiwork, created in Christ Jesus to do good works, which God prepared in advance for us to do."
> (Ephesians 2:10)

He has already planned out all your "accomplishments" and all your "good works" that you will do for Him. You cannot let Him down.

Third, God is patient, infinite, and eternal. The Scriptures tell us God is infinite, He is without measure and without end. They also tell us that He is patient. If God is infinite and patient, then He is infinitely patient with us. Disappointment infers a lack of patience.

God is also eternal. He sees all events, (past, present, and future) equally vivid. To God, long periods of time are not experienced as they are to us. We may be tempted to think that God's patience is stretched when we continue to struggle with some issue in our lives for an extended period of time. But God does not get "tired" of our failings; He does not view them in the same time frames we do.

Fourth, to suggest that our sins disappoint God is to fail to appreciate His full work at the cross. When Christ absorbed your sins into Himself, He saw clearly every sin you would ever commit. He saw it all. He knew exactly what you would do and fail to do. He saw your sins and forgave them. In fact, God knows all the lousy things you're *still going to do* and has already taken care of them at the cross.

The cross and the New Covenant changes everything.

> "For if those who live by law are heirs, faith has no value
> and the promise is worthless, because law brings wrath.
> And where there is no law there is no transgression."
> (Romans 4:14-15)

For those who no longer live under the law, there is no transgression, because of their forgiveness by the cross of Christ.

It only stands to reason, if God's wrath has been fully satisfied at the cross, so has the possibility of disappointing Him. In *Comforts from the Cross*, Elyse Fitzpatrick explains it this way:

> "Here's a gospel truth that is just astounding and meant to comfort your guilty, burdened soul: because Jesus Christ perfectly obeyed every facet of the law in your place and then died bearing all the guilt and wrath that was rightfully yours, you are no longer obligated to obey the law as a way to avoid His wrath. God has already poured out every drop of His wrath on His Son in your place. You are no longer subject to wrath, because wrath is the result of transgression or sin, and sins can be committed only when there is a law that has been violated. So now, if you're in Christ, there is no law that you can break that will bring God's punitive wrath upon you, or, as Paul put it, 'Where there is no law there is no transgression' and hence, no 'wrath.'"

Fifth, we now have the ability to enter into God's rest because of what Christ did for us on the cross. Most believers never fully realize this vitally important truth in their own lives. But the truth is, since Christ has presented His once-and-for-all sacrifice for us, we no longer need to fear when we sin.

We need not fear condemnation or even disappointment because of the cross. We no longer need to worry about displeasing Him by falling short, disappointing Him, or exhausting His patience with us. We can now enter into His rest and join Him there.

> "Day after day every priest stands and performs his religious
> duties; again and again he offers the same sacrifices, which

can never take away sins. But when this priest (Jesus) had offered for all time one sacrifice for sins, He sat down at the right hand of God. Because by one sacrifice He has made perfect forever those who are being made holy."
(Hebrews 10:11-12, 14)

During the Old Testament period, the Temple had no chairs for the priest to rest — because their job was *never* done. But because of Christ's sacrifice, we can enter into God's rest; we no longer need to strive to please God or to continually win and re-win His favor.

Sixth, God realizes that you're incapable of doing anything good on your own. Paul wrote of this often in his letter to the Romans.

"For I know that good itself does not dwell in me,
that is, in my sinful nature. For I have the desire
to do what is good, but I cannot carry it out."
(Romans 7:18)

We all try in our own power to do good, but the efforts of our flesh will always fall short of pleasing God. He doesn't expect anything good to come from our own efforts, and we set ourselves up for failure when we try. Jesus said it Himself:

"apart from Me you can do nothing."
(John 15:5)

God is patient, forgiving, merciful, and gracious. He is also a God of justice and wrath, but those qualities no longer apply to those whose sins are forgiven and atoned for through the cross. The reality is, those who are saved and have had their sins atoned for do not have to worry about His wrath — the price is already paid.

Like a good father, He will discipline us, and He will let us experience consequences in order to teach us how to live in a manner worthy of our calling. But He does not do this in anger or with a sense of disappointment. He does this because He sees who we are in Christ. He sees as holy and acceptable; as children, heirs, saints, and priests.

If this perspective tempts you to go out and sin, you're missing the point. God's grace teaches us who we are and then motivates and enables us to live like righteous children. But, when we do fail, it never surprises Him. We can never disappoint Him in the midst of our ongoing and continual process of growing to be more like Him.

Elyse Fitzpatrick, *Comforts from the Cross* (Crossway, 2009) p.20

Extra Stuff: God is Relational
Hearing God in Prayer

"This is what the Lord says, 'He who made the earth,
the Lord who formed it and established it, the Lord is
His name: Call to Me and I will answer you and tell
you great and unsearchable things you do not know.'"
Jeremiah 33:2-3

Most often, prayer is only a time of talking *to* God. Relational prayer is taking time to ask God to speak back to you. The best relationships we have are the ones where we can share honestly with one another. God desires a relationship where He not only hears from you, but you also hear from Him as well.

Questions you may find helpful to ask God in times of relational prayer:

1. God, is there any lie about me that I have believed, and what is the truth?

2. God, is there any lie about You that I have believed?

3. God, when You look at me, what do You see?

4. God, is there anything You would like me to give to You? And what do You promise to give me in return?

5. God, is there anything You want to correct in me? Or anything I need to ask forgiveness for?

6. God, what has pleased You about me lately?

7. God, is there someone who needs to be encouraged? Who?

8. God, is there something You've been saying a long time to me that You want to remind me of?

9. God, is there something new to which You are calling me?

10. God, what are You asking me to do right now?

Extra Stuff: The Trinity

The most difficult thing about the Trinity is that there is no way to perfectly and completely understand it. The Bible teaches that the Father is God, that Jesus is God, and that the Holy Spirit is God. The Bible also teaches that there is only one God.

Though we can understand some facts about the relationship of the different Persons of the Trinity, ultimately, it is incomprehensible to the human mind. However, this does not mean the Trinity is not true or that it is not based on the teachings of the Bible.

1) **There is one God** (Deuteronomy 6:4; 1 Corinthians 8:4; Galatians 3:20; 1 Timothy 2:5).

2) **The Trinity consists of three Persons** (Genesis 1:1, 26; 3:22; 11:7; Isaiah 6:8, 48:16, 61:1; Matthew 3:16-17, 28:19; 2 Corinthians 13:14). In Genesis 1:1, the Hebrew plural noun *Elohim* is used. In Genesis 1:26, 3:22, 11:7, and Isaiah 6:8, the plural pronoun for *us* is used. The word *Elohim* and the pronoun *us* are plural forms, definitely referring in the Hebrew language to more than two. While this is not an explicit argument for the Trinity, it does denote the aspect of plurality in God.

In Isaiah 48:16 and 61:1, the Son is speaking while making reference to the Father and the Holy Spirit. Compare Isaiah 61:1 to Luke 4:14-19 to see that it is the Son speaking. Matthew 3:16-17 describes the event of Jesus' baptism. Seen in this passage is God the Holy Spirit descending on God the Son while God the Father proclaims His pleasure in the Son. Matthew 28:19 and 2 Corinthians 13:14 are also examples of three distinct Persons in the Trinity.

3) **The members of the Trinity are distinguished one from another in various passages**. In the Old Testament, the Lord has a Son (Psalm 2:7, 12; Proverbs 30:2-4). The Spirit is distinguished from the "Lord" (Numbers 27:18) and from "God" (Psalm 51:10-12). God the Son is distinguished from God the Father (Psalm 45:6-7; Hebrews 1:8-9). In the New Testament, Jesus speaks to the Father about sending a Helper, the Holy Spirit (John 14:16-17).

This shows that Jesus did not consider Himself to be the Father or the Holy Spirit. Consider also all the other times in the Gospels where Jesus speaks to the Father. Was He speaking to Himself? No. He spoke to another Person in the Trinity – the Father.

4) **Each member of the Trinity is God.** The Father is God (John 6:27; Romans 1:7; 1 Peter 1:2). The Son is God (John 1:1, 14; Romans 9:5; Colossians 2:9; Hebrews 1:8; 1 John 5:20). The Holy Spirit is God (Acts 5:3-4; 1 Corinthians 3:16).

5) **The individual members of the Trinity have different tasks.** The Father is the ultimate source or cause of the universe (1 Corinthians 8:6; Revelation 4:11); divine revelation (Revelation 1:1); salvation (John 3:16-17); and Jesus' human works (John 5:17; 14:10). The Father initiates all of these things.

The Son is the agent through whom the Father does the following works: the creation and maintenance of the universe (1 Corinthians 8:6; John 1:3; Colossians 1:16-17); divine revelation (John 1:1, 16:12-15; Matthew 11:27; Revelation 1:1); and salvation (2 Corinthians 5:19; Matthew 1:21; John 4:42). The Father does all these things through the Son, who functions as His agent.

The Holy Spirit is the means by whom the Father does the following works: creation and maintenance of the universe (Genesis 1:2; Job 26:13; Psalm 104:30); divine revelation (John 16:12-15; Ephesians 3:5; 2 Peter 1:21); salvation (John 3:6; Titus 3:5; 1 Peter 1:2); and Jesus' works (Isaiah 61:1; Acts 10:38). Thus, the Father does all these things by the power of the Holy Spirit.

All Illustrations Ultimately Fail
There have been many attempts to develop practical illustrations to help explain the Trinity. However, none are completely accurate. Some have said the Trinity is like an egg. An egg is made up out of three distinct parts; the yolk, the whites, and the shell.

But the egg illustration fails in that the shell, the whites, and yolk are *parts* of the egg, not the egg in themselves. The Father, Son, and Holy Spirit are not parts of God; each of them *is* God.

The water illustration is somewhat better, but it still fails to adequately describe the Trinity. Liquid, vapor, and ice are forms of water. The Father, Son, and Holy Spirit are not forms of God, each of them is God. So, while these illustrations may give us a picture of the Trinity, the picture is not entirely accurate.

The bottom line is this: An infinite God cannot be fully described by a finite illustration. There is a mystery about the Trinity that we need to simply embrace – instead of try to figure out and fully comprehend.

Why the Trinity is a BIG DEAL

The Trinity proves that God is Relational. For all eternity God has existed in relationship with Himself. There is one God, who exists in three persons. "The Trinity means that God is, in essence, relational." ' He is not an impersonal force or even an unipersonal being.

The Trinity proves that God is Loving. Because God is relational, He is also loving. You cannot have love (or be a loving being) if you are all alone without someone else to love.

> "If God is unipersonal, then until God created other beings there was no love, since love is something that one person has for another. This means that a unipersonal God was power, sovereignty, and greatness from all eternity, but not love." '

If God was just one person, He could not be loving for all eternity.

The Trinity proves that God is Happy. God asks us to praise Him, glorify Him and center our lives around Him, because He wants our joy. When you love someone, you want them to be happy. God wants us to be happy, but realizes that our happiness can only be truly found when we center our lives on a happy God.

> "He has infinite happiness not through self-centeredness, but through self-giving, other-centered love. And the only way we, who have been created in His image, can have the same joy, is if we center our lives around Him instead of ourselves." '

God's glory is His primary concern, but His love for us is "others oriented" because He desires to share His glory and His joy with us.

The Trinity proves that God is Humble. Each person of the Trinity exists to bring glory to the others. There is an "other orientation" at the center of God's being.

> "The life of the Trinity is characterized not by self-centeredness but by mutually self-giving love... Each of the divine persons centers upon the others. None demands that the others revolve around Him. Each voluntarily circles the other two, pouring love, delight, and adoration into them. Each person of the Trinity loves, adores, defers to, and rejoices in the others. That creates a dynamic, pulsating dance of joy and love." '

The Trinity shows us quite clearly that God's relational, loving, happy and humble attributes are all related and actually feed off of one another. The three persons of the Trinity display for us the perfect working out of these characteristics.

Edited and Amended from GotAnswers.org - http://www.gotquestions.org/Trinity-Bible.html - September 23rd, 2010
* The four BIG DEAL quotes are taken from *The Reason for God* by Timothy Keller (pages 223-227)

ENDNOTES:

Our Biggest Problem

1 – A.W. Tozer, *The Knowledge of the Holy* (Harper, 1961) p. 4
2 – Tozer, p. 43
3 – Tozer, p. 8

Solutions and Rewards

1 – Tozer, p. 1
2 – Brennan Manning, *Ruthless Trust* (Harper, 2000) p. 57
3 – Manning, p. 56
4 – Tozer, p. 2-3

1. God is Infinite

1 – Tozer, p. 45
2 – R.C. Sproul, *Essential Truths of the Christian Faith* (Tyndale, 1992) p. 31-32
3 – Grudem, *Systematic Theology*, (Zondervan, 1994) p. 167
4 – Grudem, *Systematic Theology*, p. 167
5 – Tozer, p. 46

2. God is Holy

1 – Tozer, p. 104
2 – Paul Tripp, *Broken Down House* (Shepherd Press, 2009) p. 103
3 – Tozer, p. 103
4 – Tozer, p. 104
5 – Sproul, p. 47
6 – Wayne Grudem, *Essential Teachings of the Christian Faith*, (Zondervan, 1999) p. 254
7 – Tozer, p. 107
8 – Arthur Pink, *The Attributes of God* (Baker, 1975) p. 57

3. God is Loving

1 – Tozer, p. 97
2 – Tozer, p. 98
3 – Tozer, p. 98
4 – Grudem, *Systematic Theology*, p. 199
5 – J.I. Packer, *Knowing God* (InterVarsity Press, 1973) p. 113
6 – Pink, p. 99-103
7 – Grudem, *Systematic Theology*, p. 198-199
8 – Packer, p. 114

4. God is Merciful

1 – Tozer, p. 90-91
2 – Tozer, p. 91
3 – Pink, p. 92
4 – Pink, p. 93
5 – Pink, p. 93
6 – Tozer, p. 91
7 – Grudem, *Systematic Theology*, p. 200
8 – Tozer, p. 92

5. God is Gracious

1 – Tozer, p. 97
2 – Tozer, p. 98
3 – Tozer, p. 95
4 – Pink, p. 85
5 – Packer, p. 120
6 – Pink, p. 85
7 – Pink, p. 86-87
8 – Timothy Keller, *The Reason for God* (Riverhead Books, 2008) p. 189
9 – Grudem, *Systematic Theology*, p. 201
10 – Grudem, *Systematic Theology*, p. 201
11 – Charles Spurgeon, *Memorial Library*, Vol. XIV (Zondervan, no publication date) p. 325

6. God is Righteous

1 – The Simpson's (Season 2), writer: Steve Pepoon, 2/7/91
2 – Tozer, p. 86
3 – Grudem, *Systematic Theology*, p. 203
4 – Tozer, p. 87
5 – Tozer, p. 87-88
6 – Tozer, p. 88
7 – Pink, p. 106
8 – Pink, p. 106
9 – Grudem, *Systematic Theology*, p. 204
10 – Grudem, *Systematic Theology*, p. 204
11 – Pink, p. 107
12 – Tozer, p. 89
13 – Keller, *A Reason for God*, p. 74
14 – Packer, p. 138
15 – Tozer, p. 89
16 – Grudem, *Systematic Theology*, p. 205
17 – Chris Tiegreen, *The One Year Walk with God Devotional* (Tyndale, 2004) p. 163
18 – Spurgeon, p. 330
19 – Francis Chan, *Erasing Hell*, (David C. Cook, 2011) p. 17
20 – Chan, *Erasing Hell*, p. 141

7. God is All Present

1 – Tozer, p. 74
2 – Sproul, p. 43
3 – Grudem, *Systematic Theology*, p. 175

8. God is All Powerful

1 – Mark Batterson, *In a Pit with a Lion on a Snowy Day* (Multnomah, 2006) p. 33
2 – Tozer, p. 67
3 – Tozer, p. 65
4 – Tozer, p. 65
5 – Pink, p. 58
6 – Grudem, *Systematic Theology*, p. 217
7 – Tozer, p. 66
8 – Tozer, p. 66
9 – Sproul, p. 40

9. God is All Knowing

1 – Pink, p. 21
2 – Tozer, p. 55
3 – Tozer, p. 56
4 – Pink, p. 23
5 – Grudem, *Systematic Theology*, p. 192
6 – Tiegreen, p. 133
7 – Pink, p. 22

10. God is Transcendent

1 – Tozer, p. 71
2 – Tozer, p. 70
3 – Manning, p. 50
4 – Manning, p. 76
5 – Manning, p. 77
6 – Packer, p. 73
7 – Manning, p. 77

11. God is Unchanging

1 – Grudem, *Systematic Theology*, p. 163
2 – Tozer, p. 49
3 – Pink, p. 46
4 – Grudem, *Systematic Theology*, p. 168
5 – Tozer, p. 51

6 – Pink, p. 49
7 – Tozer, p.53
8 – Packer, p. 70

12. God is Sovereign

1 – Jerry Bridges, *Trusting God* (NavPress, 1998) p. 34
2 – Pink, p. 40
3 – Pink, p. 40
4 – John Piper, *Spectacular Sins* (Crossway, 2008) p. 30
5 – Piper, *Spectacular Sins,* p. 17
6 – Richard Brody, (ed.) *If I Had Only One Sermon to Preach*, (Baker Books, 1994) p. 219-220
7 – Brody, p. 220
8 – Mark Batterson, *Wild Goose Chase* (Multnomah, 2008) p. 4
9 – C.S. Lewis, *The Problem of Pain*, (HarperCollins, 1996) p. 91
10 – Bridges, p. 73-74

13. God is Self-Existent

1 – Sproul, p. 37
2 – Tozer, p. 25
3 – Tozer, p. 26
4 – Tozer, p. 26
5 – Tozer, p. 27
6 – Sproul, p. 38
7 – Tozer, p. 27-28

14. God is Self-Sufficient

1 – Tozer, p. 32
2 – Tozer, p. 33
3 – Tozer, p. 34
4 – Pink, p. 10

15. God is Wise

1 – Grudem, *Systematic Theology,* p. 193
2 – Tozer, p. 63
3 – Grudem, *Systematic Theology,* p. 193
4 – Tiegreen, p.104
5 – Tozer, p. 59
6 – Tiegreen, p. 57
7 – Tiegreen, p. 87
8 – Tozer, p. 60
9 – Tozer, p. 63
10 – Tiegreen, p.127
11 – Grudem, *Systematic Theology,* p. 194
12 – Tiegreen, p. 208

16. God is Faithful

1 – Grudem, *Systematic Theology,* p. 195
2 – Keller, *A Reason for God*, p. xvii
3 – Tiegreen, p. 115
4 – Tozer, p. 78
5 – Pink, p. 67
6 – Oswald Chambers, *My Utmost for His Highest* (Discovery House Publishers, 1935) Oct. 23rd
7 – Tiegreen, p.138
8 – Tripp, p. 49-50
9 – Tiegreen, p. 213

17. God is Good

1 – Tozer, p. 82
2 – Bridges, p.23
3 – Grudem, *Systematic Theology,* p. 197
4 – Grudem, *Systematic Theology,* p. 197
5 – Pink, p. 74
6 – Pink, p. 75

7 – Pink, p. 76
8 – Grudem, *Systematic Theology*, p. 198
9 – Tiegreen, p. 172
10 – Bridges, p. 145
11 – Francis Chan, *Forgotten God* (David C. Cook, 2009) p. 83
12 – Tozer, p. 82
13 – Tozer, p. 84
14 – Grudem, *Systematic Theology*, p. 198
15 – Sproul, p. 149

19. God is Eternal
1 – Tozer, p. 39
2 – Tozer, p. 39
3 – Grudem, *Systematic Theology*, p. 168
4 – Grudem, *Systematic Theology*, p. 169
5 – Grudem, *Systematic Theology*, p. 172

20. God is Jealous
1 – Grudem, *Systematic Theology*, p. 205
2 – C.S. Lewis, *The Weight of Glory* (Eerdmans, 1965) p. 1-2
3 – Timothy Keller, *Counterfeit Gods*, (Dutton, 2009) p. 17

21. God is Humble
1 – Tiegreen, p. 156
2 – Jonathan Edwards, *Some Thoughts Concerning the Present Revival of Religion in New England* (1742), Part IV, Section I

22. God is Patient
1 – Millard Erickson, *Christian Theology* (Baker Books, 1985) p. 296
2 – Erickson, p. 296
3 – Pink, p. 80
4 – Pink, p. 80
5 – Pink, p. 81
6 – Bridges, p. 121
7 – Grudem, *Systematic Theology*, p. 201

23. God is Truth
1 – Grudem, *Systematic Theology*, p. 195
2 – Grudem, *Systematic Theology*, p. 195
3 – Erickson, p. 291
4 – Grudem, *Systematic Theology*, p. 196
5 – Grudem, *Systematic Theology*, p. 196
6 – Ravi Zacharias, Address to the United Nations Prayer Breakfast, September 10th 2002.
7 – Grudem, *Systematic Theology*, p. 197

24. God is Happy
1 – John Piper, *The Pleasures of God*, (Multnomah, 2000) p. 26
2 – Tozer, p. 33
3 – John Piper, *Desiring God*, (Multnomah, 1996) p. 40
4 – Grudem, *EssentialTeachings* p. 99
5 – Piper, *Desiring God*, p. 41-42
6 – Blaise Pascal, *Pascal's Pensées*, trans. By W.F.Trotter (Dutton, 1958), p. 113
7 – Piper, *Desiring God*, p. 33

25. God is Relational
1 – Newkirk, *The Washington Times*, August 29th, 1999
2 – Grudem, *Systematic Theology*, p. 443
3 – Grudem, *Systematic Theology*, p. 443
4 – Grudem, *Systematic Theology*, p. 167
5 – Tiegreen, p. 224

It Makes a Difference
1 – John Piper, *When I Don't Desire God*, (Crossway, 2004) p. 30-31